# THE ROMANS

OTHER BOOKS ABOUT MAJOR CULTURES OF THE WORLD

*Seafarers of the Pacific*, by Douglas Newton

*The Northmen*, by Thomas Caldecot Chubb

*Horsemen of the Steppes*, by Walter A. Fairservis, Jr.

*Slavic Peoples*, by Thomas Caldecot Chubb

*Land of the Two Rivers*, by Leonard Cottrell

*The Peoples of Africa*, by Colin M. Turnbull

*The Incas, People of the Sun*, by Victor W. von Hagen

*Land of the Pharaohs*, by Leonard Cottrell

*India*, by Walter A. Fairservis, Jr.

*Maya, Land of the Turkey and the Deer*, by Victor W. von Hagen

*The Chinese Way of Life*, by Lin Yutang

*The Byzantines*, by Thomas Caldecot Chubb

*The Arabs*, by Harry B. Ellis

*The Sun Kingdom of the Aztecs*, by Victor W. von Hagen

# THE
# ROMANS

## BY ALFRED DUGGAN

ILLUSTRATED BY *Richard M. Powers*

## THE WORLD PUBLISHING COMPANY
NEW YORK

32,601

Published by The World Publishing Company
110 East 59th Street, New York, New York 10022

Published simultaneously in Canada by
Nelson, Foster & Scott Ltd.

Library of Congress catalog card number: 64-13513
Seventh Printing August 1971

5WP67

# CONTENTS

# THE ROMANS

# THE BEGINNING

Once, long ago, the river Tiber in Italy was the boundary between two very different peoples. The men who lived on the west bank believed that their ancestors had come by sea from Asia Minor, bringing with them a strange, magical religion. They knew how to work iron mines and marble quarries; in return for exports of these products they imported Greek vases and pictures, and copied them, rather clumsily, to adorn their own cities. Because they knew so much magic their neighbors considered them uncanny and frightening. Their language has perished, so we do not know what they called themselves. The rest of Italy called them the Etruscans.

On the east bank, in what is for mountainous Italy a wide plain, lived a race of industrious farmers, who took it for granted that their ancestors had lived there always. They were a practical, down-to-earth people, not given to flights of fancy; so they called themselves just the Latins, the men of the wide plain.

Among the Latins lived two young men, twins, named Romulus and Remus. Through their mother they were descended from Aeneas, the Trojan hero who fled to Italy when the Greeks sacked his city; he had brought with him some of the Sacred Things of Troy, especially the Palladium, the very ancient, very holy wooden image of the goddess Pallas Athena. But it was believed that the father of the twins was the war god Mars.

These young men decided to found a new city on the east bank of the Tiber, on the very border of the Etruscans; but they disagreed about the exact site until the superior magic of Romulus prevailed. Romulus was full of Good Luck and highly skilled in magic. With a white bull and a white cow yoked to his plow he began to trace a furrow where the walls of his city would rise. He did it with many prayers and spells; when he came to a place where a gate would be made he lifted the plowshare. For in a magical sense this furrow was already the wall of the city, and it must be filled with a spell that would stop any foe from crossing it.

But while he plowed, his twin brother Remus, out of mere spite and jealousy, jumped over the furrow and thus spoiled all the magic in it.

Romulus might have begun again somewhere else, which was what Remus wanted. Instead, he killed Remus on the spot. Thus, by the sacrifice of a man, which was already rare in those days—and that man his closest kin, his twin brother—he strengthened enormously the magic in the furrow. The city thus founded must become strong and mighty, as indeed it did. It endures to this day, and it has always been called Rome after Romulus, its founder.

We know exactly when this happened, for the birthday of Rome has never been forgotten. It was April 21, 753 B.C.

The new city was one among many; twelve others lay in the Latin plain, and among the Etruscans they were numerous. It was ruled as were most other cities of that time. The king, Romulus, led the army and judged law suits, but his most important duty was to keep on good terms with the gods by offering sacrifice on behalf of the whole people.

The gods could be pleased only by sacrifice, never by the righteous conduct of their worshipers. There were usually reckoned to be twelve great gods, headed by Jupiter and his wife Juno. But the number of minor divinities was nearly infinite, and all must be placated. Every grove, every spring, was ruled by its god, and if you did not know his name you must still sacrifice to him with the correct ritual. Roman gods were bare supernatural forces, very little more than names. Unlike the Greeks, the early Romans did not tell stories about their exploits or invent for them an elaborate family life.

If you offered sacrifice correctly to the gods, at the time when sacrifice was due to them, they would do you no harm. That was the best you could expect. No pagan Roman loved a god or supposed that a god could love him.

The chief civic duty of a Roman was not to pay taxes, but

to take his place in the ranks of the army. Every citizen must bring at least a shield and a spear, and if he could also bring armor and a sword he would be more welcome, and safer.

But it is foolish to go to war if the army is unwilling to fight; so whenever the citizens mustered in arms the king would ask them whether they approved of the campaign. A man's vote was valued according to his military worth; a fully armed spearman could outvote several archers or slingers, and a mounted man—a knight—could outvote several good spearmen.

The king had in addition his special advisers, the heads of great families or old men chosen for their wisdom. Collectively, this council of advisers was known as the Senate (the Old Men).

Under King Romulus the city flourished, because he welcomed settlers from any quarter. His own followers were Latins, but he made a treaty with a group of Sabines from the hills, who joined him as an organized unit under their own king; and he gave refuge to fugitives from anywhere, without inquiring why they had left home. During his reign the Romans were divided into three tribes: Latins, Sabines, and all the rest. In early Rome it did not matter where you came from, so long as you were a good citizen.

What really bound these groups together was a belief in the luck of their city. Rome, which contained the Sacred Things of mighty Troy, was especially favored by the gods. Not only had it been founded by a son of Mars, who had offered his twin brother as a foundation sacrifice; but when the settlers built their first huts on the Capitol, the citadel, they unearthed a fresh, still bleeding, human head. That must mean that Rome was destined to be the head of the whole world.

The people who believed all these things were very like us. In three thousand years the capacity of the human brain has not altered. Primitive Romans in their little primitive city were just as intelligent as their descendants of the present day. But in the ordinary affairs of life they had none of our modern machinery. The early Romans managed, but they showed a tendency to do things the hard way. They themselves were not afraid of physical toil, and from the earliest times they had slaves to help them.

Their chief food was grain, either barley or wheat, which are not the easiest crops to grow in mountainous Italy. Wherever the ground was fairly flat the Romans marked out square arable fields. The fields were square because the wooden plowshare barely scratched the earth, and to cultivate it properly the plow must go over the ground a second time, at right angles to the first. Plowing, the most important operation on the farm, was usually done by the farmer himself.

Bread was the Roman staff of life, but baking calls for a brick oven and a plentiful supply of charcoal. On campaign, therefore, or whenever they were in a hurry the Romans ate porridge. Porridge, and nothing but porridge, was the standard army ration right up to the beginning of the Empire. Once, when Julius Caesar was conquering Gaul, his hungry troops had to eat the local cattle; they grumbled at the hardship of dining on fresh beef instead of the usual porridge.

Of course the Romans also kept cattle, but they kept them to pull their plows and wagons, not for eating. After a sacrifice a small part of the beast was burned to make a meal for the god, and the rest of the carcass was eaten by the priests or the poor. But it was eaten because it was there and cost nothing, not because it was a luxury.

At feasts the Romans ate pork. Because pigs seek their food by rooting the soil they were regarded as slightly uncanny, creatures of the Underworld and the most appropriate sacrifice to the gods below.

Sheep were valued for wool, not for mutton. The official dress of a Roman citizen was a long woolen cloak, the toga; it could never be worn by foreigners or slaves. By rights the toga should have been spun and woven by the wife of its wearer. As plowing was work for a gentleman, so weaving was work for a lady. Every Roman matron should be skilled in it.

On the land, where all wagons and plows were drawn by oxen, there was no work for horses. Yet cavalry was needed in war. So horses were bought with public money and quartered on the more prosperous farms. The farmer who supplied free grazing and fodder was entitled to ride the horse in battle, with the rank of knight.

Roman farmers, tilling their square fields, liked everything about them to be square. Rome was a square city, divided by straight streets into blocks of square houses. Roman temples were square platforms, open to the sky. There might be a hut to shelter the image of the god; but the platform was essentially the workshop of the diviner, who partitioned the sky above him into imaginary squares and foretold the future by noting in which squares birds appeared.

In this square city, where the only round building was the shrine of Vesta, the goddess who guarded the common hearth of the city, there was very little culture. The early Romans composed excellent laws; they did not compose anything else—no poetry, no history, no mythology. Their ramparts kept out the enemy, their houses kept out the weather;

there was no superfluous ornament. They never carved in stone. If an image of a god was needed it was made from terra cotta, clay baked in a mold and then painted. Accuracy of form was here more important than beauty; Janus, the god of boundaries and of the new year, must show his two faces, gazing forward and back. If he did not look especially godlike that did not matter.

These hard-working, practical, prosaic farmers excelled in only two things: they lived together in a crowded city without quarreling, and when they went to war they fought so gallantly that they usually won.

There were in all seven kings of Rome, whose reigns fill the years 753–509 B.C. They seem to have been chosen by the people without any strict hereditary claim, though sometimes the new king was connected by marriage with the family of his predecessor.

The seventh king, Tarquin the Proud, was an Etruscan. About the time of his election an aristocracy of Etruscans held sway over much of Italy, and some historians have assumed that the coming of this Etruscan king denotes an Etruscan conquest. But later Romans stoutly denied that anyone had ever conquered them. The election of Tarquin may have been a coincidence.

The Romans drew a sharp distinction between public and private life. In public they obeyed the law and submitted to the will of the majority, but in private the head of each household demanded unfettered freedom. In each household only the head was truly free. He held as much power over his wife and children as over his slaves. At marriage a father's absolute power over his daughter was formally given to her husband. Every woman was always in the power of some man; a widow might be subject to her eldest son.

The head of the household might do as he wished with his own.

Tarquin the Proud, and even more so his impudent son Sextus, trespassed on the private lives of the Romans by making love to their wives. So in the year 509 B.C. the Romans rebelled, chased Tarquin back to Etruria, and defeated the Etruscan army which tried to restore him.

After getting rid of their kings, the Romans decided they must devise a republican constitution. They disliked innovation, so they built on what remained to them: the assembly of all the citizens, known as the Comitia, and the Senate of veteran councilors. These two bodies could make new laws, but in a time of perpetual war they needed one man at the top, to give orders to the army.

But one man at the top would be very like a king, and even if he were elected for a limited term of office he might gather so many supporters that he could not be dislodged when his term was ended. So the Comitia deliberately elected two equal consuls, to hold office for a single year.

The consuls did not rule jointly. Each consul was supreme, and his commands must be obeyed unless they were countermanded by the other equal consul. Even an unlawful command must be obeyed without question, at the time; but at the end of the year the ex-consul, now a private citizen, must answer to the people for all his illegal actions. Such a double supreme command must end in frustration and chaos unless both consuls exercised forbearance and common sense. In fact it worked quite well, because forbearance and common sense were virtues in which the Romans were pre-eminent.

The most frequent duty of a consul was to lead the army in battle. To help him in this task the Comitia elected subordinate officials, praetors, also for one year only. The lowest grade of elected officials were the aediles, who looked after temples and other public buildings.

But all these officials had another important duty; they must watch the flight of birds to find out what luck had in store for the Roman people. The Latin word for this bird-watching was *auspicium*. It was, of course, as futile as astrology or any other attempt to foretell the future; but, like astrology, it was governed by certain rules. The appearance of this bird always presaged good fortune, the appearance of that one bad. But at once the practical-minded Romans saw a difficulty.

Birds were sent by the gods to indicate the future. The gods, however, might not always understand which question they were being asked. Apparently they could always recognize a king when they saw one, and would know that he was asking questions concerning the fate of his kingdom. But how were they to tell whether an ordinary Roman citizen was inquiring about his own personal luck or about the fortune of his city? A religious ceremony was devised, to make this clear even to a divine intelligence. The auspices of Rome, the right to learn the fortune of the whole community, were solemnly transferred to each consul and praetor and aedile at the beginning of his year of office. At the end of the year he yielded them up to his successor. As a token that these elected officials each held some of the divine character of a king, they were all provided with special thrones, decorated with plaques of ivory.

The Romans regarded ivory as a magical substance. The Latin word for ivory has no connection with the Latin (really Greek) word for elephant, which indicates that the Romans did not know what ivory was. The elephants nearest to Italy lived in north Africa, but the nearest place where they were regularly hunted was India. Little bits of carved ivory, not recognizable as tusks, drifted through the markets of the Mediterranean; the Romans were not the only people who saw them as something magical and unknown.

The men who filled these half-religious offices ought to be chosen from families which were especially skilled in pleasing the gods. As early as the beginning of the Republic there were two classes of citizens in Rome, patricians and plebeians. Patricians were much more important than plebeians, though what made them so we do not know. Perhaps they sprang from a priestly class already in existence when Rome was founded. It is not likely that they were descended from the first settlers and the plebeians from later immigrants; for the Claudii, who came to Rome in the fifth century B.C., were recognized as patrician.

The distinction was most marked in personal ways of living. Patricians married for life, a plebeian had only one wife at a time but he might change her as often as he chose. Their burial rites differed, too. The patricians were always a minority, which grew smaller since the offspring of a mixed marriage were ranked as plebeian.

In effect, although every citizen of Rome had a vote in the election of the consuls, he might vote only for a patrician. The chance of fame and glory depended to a great extent on the accident of birth.

The accident of birth always mattered in Rome. Although the theory of the constitution saw each citizen as an individual, every Roman saw himself as a member of a clan. Their names kept the clan system alive. Each citizen bore three names; the middle one, the *nomen* proper, the very emblem of citizenship, was always a clan name. Thus Julius was the name of a famous clan, so large that its various branches were distinguished by hereditary nicknames, *cognomina*, of which Caesar was one. The forename, *praenomen*, in Gaius Julius Caesar counted for little and was used only to distinguish a man from his brothers. Every time you addressed a citizen by name you reminded him of his clan; some clans were more powerful and important than others, but in politics every clan tended to support its leading members.

In the very distant past the Romans may have literally worshiped their ancestors; in historic times they paid them great reverence. They believed in a future life, but a very gloomy one. In the cold, dark Underworld the spirits of the dead wandered unhappily, envious of the living; blood spilled in sacrifice got into their veins and made them more contented with their lot, so that they did no harm. But the spirits of a man's own ancestors looked after him, as a living man looks after his sons. The tricky moment came when a man died and went to join the great majority, for his ancestors might not recognize the stranger.

Therefore a Roman funeral was a very solemn affair. The corpse was carried, exposed to view on a bier, to the pyre where it would be burned. Afterward the ashes were collected in an urn and preserved in the family tomb. In the procession marched all the living kindred and the household slaves, with hired mourners to wail around the bier. To make sure that the ancestors were also present they were impersonated. Actors walked before the corpse, wearing masks modeled on the features of the ancestors; they wore the toga, the official insignia, and the decorations that each ancestor had worn while he was on earth, all done as realistically as possible. Later a bust of the deceased, copied from the waxen mask molded on his dead face, would join the busts of earlier ancestors on the shelf where images of the household gods were worshiped. There it would receive offerings and prayers for so long as the clan should endure. Some clans practiced burial instead of cremation, and there might be changes of fashion, though cremation was more frequent. Slaves and the very poor were buried, because it was the cheaper method. The funeral oration in praise of the deceased presently became the most important part of the ceremony.

All this was officially ignored in the constitution of the Republic. But clan solidarity underlies many otherwise inexplicable political movements.

# THE EARLY REPUBLIC

It is evident, from this sketch of early Rome, that central Italy in the fifth century B.C. had little contact with the great world. About this time the Greeks were beginning their long struggle with Persia. They had evolved elaborate political institutions. In architecture, sculpture, and vase-painting they were already launched on a great career. Their literature included the Homeric poems. None of this had penetrated to Rome, though there were Greek colonists in southern Italy.

Nevertheless Rome was already a place of some importance. Under their first consuls the Romans ranked as equal partners with the confederation of twelve Latin cities, their neighbors. The allied army was made up of two roughly equal contingents, Roman and Latin; on alternate days a Roman or a Latin general took command. This allied army was continually engaged in wars of conquest, either against the civilized but decaying cities of Etruria or against the more savage hill tribes from the Apennines.

Although no documents survive from this early period, many legends were related by subsequent historians. These legends may not be exactly true; at best they are the tall stories soldiers tell after a successful campaign. But from them we can see at least the type of action the Romans thought admirable and to be remembered.

Similar Greek stories are full of clever tricks, riddles, and answers with double meanings. The Romans did not care for that kind of thing. The stories they admired were of stark courage, devotion to duty, and unflinching patriotism. Nothing must come before the citizen's duty to Rome. For instance, the story was told of the three Horatius brothers who fought a judicial duel against three Curatius brothers from Alba. Two Horatii were killed, but then the remaining brother killed all three Curatii, even though one of them was engaged to marry his sister. When she mourned her betrothed he killed her also, for lack of patriotism. For this he was condemned to death, but he appealed to the Comitia, which voted to pardon him. So was established a right of appeal which endured for centuries. Any Roman citizen condemned to death might appeal to the Comitia for pardon.

On the other hand, there is the story of the maiden Tarpeia, who for greed of gold agreed to betray Rome to the Sabines. The Sabines took advantage of her treachery and then pelted her to death with their shields; for treason is so abhorrent that even those who gain by it cannot be trusted to keep faith with the traitor. In the end the body of the wicked girl was thrown down a cliff and left unburied. As the Romans attached great importance to a seemly burial, it was doubtful whether the spirit of an unburied corpse could find rest in the next world, though a very rough and ready token burial was enough to satisfy the gods. (Even after a lost battle the beaten commander was supposed to beg for a truce to bury his dead.)

The virtuous maiden Cloelia swam the flooded Tiber to

escape from her foes. The gallant youth Scaevola held his hand in the flames without flinching, to prove to the wicked Etruscans that he would always be their enemy. When a chasm opened in the Forum, the market place of Rome, and the soothsayers declared that the gods would not close it until the Romans had thrown in their most valuable possession, the good knight Curtius jumped in fully armed and mounted. Of course the chasm closed at once, for the gods agreed that a good soldier was the most valuable thing Rome possessed. And Brutus, when consul commanding the army, condemned his own sons to death for disobedience to orders; in an army discipline must come before family feeling.

Courage, patriotism, unswerving public spirit which could not be influenced by private affection—these were the qualities the Romans most admired. There is in many of these stories another quality, harder to define: a dislike of personal pomposity coupled with a reverence for official rank. A war against the Aequii was going so badly that the Senate decided to offer supreme command to an eminent general named Cincinnatus. A deputation of senators found him plowing on his farm, stripped to the waist. He put on his toga before he heard what they had to say, for a citizen should wear official dress when taking part in official business. Cincinnatus took over the army and beat the Aequii. Then he went back to his farm, stripped again to the waist, and finished his plowing. He expected no honor or precedence for doing his patriotic duty, and certainly he was no richer than before.

The office assumed by Cincinnatus was that of Dictator, which was filled only in a grave emergency, for example if both consuls had been killed in battle or had confessed themselves incompetent to conduct the war. For six months and not a day longer the Romans would submit to the rule of a single man; when his period of command was over the ex-Dictator must step down into the ranks again.

Curius Dentatus was an influential senator, though in private life he happened to be very poor. One day, while he was busy cooking his dinner, an embassy of foreigners, Samnites, called on him. He cooked his own dinner because he could not afford a slave-cook, and the dinner was of vegetables only because he could not afford pork. The Samnites had brought a great treasure of gold, with which they hoped to bribe Dentatus into supporting a treaty favorable to them. Dentatus refused the bribe, and explained his conduct very simply. "Which is the more honorable," he asked, "to possess gold, or to give orders to those who possess it?"

That was the kind of story that the head of a Roman household told to his admiring and obedient family, as they sat together by the fire in the evening. The fire was the soul of a Roman house. It was never permitted to go out, partly because of the bother of rekindling it with flint and steel; and as it smoldered day and night it provided a home for the good fairies, the *lares*, who guarded the family luck. In a properly lucky household another family of good fairies, the *penates*, lived in the storeroom to make sure that it was never empty. Since the Romans had not learned how to build chimneys, smoke from the fire blackened the whole living room, which was therefore called the *atrium*. In it on a shelf stood the images of the household gods, with the ancestors beside them; every day the head of the household prayed to them, on behalf of the whole family.

Though most Romans were farmers, they lived in the city and walked out to their fields every morning, as do many

Italian peasants at the present day. If the farm lay so far off that it was beyond walking distance of the city, the farmer could take no part in public life. To vote in the Comitia the citizen had to be physically present in the Forum; not even the Greeks had yet hit on the idea of electing representatives to vote for men who were busy earning their living.

The laborious and inefficient Roman method of tilling the soil did not occupy the whole year. In the spring the farmer had to plow and sow, in the autumn he had to reap the harvest. But in the summer the crop could be left in the ground

to grow by itself. That was when the farmer marched off to conquer more plowland from his neighbors.

For some reason which we cannot now explain, these hard-headed, practical Philistine farmers fought better than their neighbors. By the year 400 B.C. Rome ruled all Latium and Etruria and much of the Apennine hill country. It was an empire in miniature, and the Romans had already mastered some of their characteristic methods of ruling an empire.

Rome ruled with astonishing tact and moderation. In those days every little city fought desperately against invasion, for if the invaders got in, the city would be sacked and its people enslaved. There was no halfway house between complete independence and abject servitude, until the Romans invented one.

Rome controlled only the foreign policy of a conquered city. The citizens must fight under Roman command, but at home they might manage their own affairs. Most of these cities were linked with Rome by two valued privileges: *commercium*, by which contracts made in either place would be enforced by the courts of the other; *connubium*, by which the children of a mixed marriage took the citizenship of the father. Hitherto it had been impossible to enforce a contract against a foreigner, and if a man married a foreign wife his children would have no native city. Note that two conquered cities were never linked by *commercium* and *connubium;* Rome remained the only center of the web.

But no free man of another city was enslaved, and no conquered city paid tribute. The obligation to serve in a victorious Roman army was not irksome. Very soon these conquered Italians were proud to be the subject allies of Rome.

But while Rome prospered abroad there was strife at home. Money was coming into the city; foreign money, of course, for the Romans minted no coins except clumsy lumps of copper. The simple farmer-citizens could not cope with it.

Thus it had been in Athens and many other ancient cities of which we have record. The arrival of gold and silver, in quantities enough to form a currency, upset the economy. Farmers are always borrowing from their neighbors, an ox to make up the plowteam, a measure of seed. After the harvest has been gathered it is easy to return the loan, with something extra to requite the kindness. But it is fatally easy to borrow silver, and very difficult to pay it back.

The Roman law of debt was severe. There was no escape by declaring bankruptcy. If a man owed more than he could pay he must be sold into slavery, with his wife and children, to satisfy his creditors. Various temporary measures were enacted to meet a particular crisis, but the problem of in-solvent debtors was never settled while the Republic lasted. Whenever a free Roman was enslaved for debt there was an outcry, but no one could think of any better way of doing justice to his creditors.

The arrival of money brought another strain to the social structure. At this early date it is absurd to talk of rich and poor; as yet there were no wealthy Romans. But some farmers were better off than others, and in general patricians owned more land than plebeians. Now some plebeians began to prosper in trade until they were richer than their betters. Yet they were debarred by their birth from public office, which was the ambition of every self-respecting Roman.

We cannot disentangle what actually happened from the many legends told about it. But it appears that on two separate occasions the plebeians threatened a general strike, a typically Roman way of bringing pressure to bear; they threatened to abandon Rome and found a new plebeian city of their own. Out of patriotism the patricians gave way. In fact the plebeians won hands down.

The constitution was changed to make plebeians eligible for every office. In addition it was decreed that one consul must always be a plebeian, though there was no law that the other must be a patrician. An assembly of plebeians, from which patricians were excluded, could pass decrees— plebiscites—binding on the whole city.

The plebeians also elected, to protect their interests, officials called tribunes. A tribune did not receive the auspices; so he might not use the throne decorated with sacred ivory which was the mark of a true Roman magistrate or offer sacrifice to the gods on behalf of the Roman people. But his person was declared sacred, so that to harm him was a grave sacrilege; and though he might not give orders he could forbid any action whatsoever. If a law was about to be passed, if a citizen was about to be punished, any tribune might say *veto* (I forbid), and no further action could be taken. Like every other Roman official, the tribunes were elected annually and held office for one year.

Henceforth a plebeian had a better chance of a political career than a patrician, so that occasionally an ambitious young patrician sought adoption into a plebeian family. But in everything connected with religion patricians came first, and socially they were envied and respected by those of lesser birth.

By about the year 400 B.C. Rome ruled most of central Italy. Then all was ruined by foreign invasion. The Romans had to begin again at the beginning—which they did, quite undismayed.

Gauls, huge fair-haired barbarians, taller and more war-like than any Italian, had spread over the Alps into northern Italy. After occupying the valley of the Po they were now pressing south through the Apennines. They were comparative newcomers; when Rome was founded there were no Gauls in Italy.

The legends, which are our only sources for this period, show these barbarians as behaving in a surprisingly sophisticated fashion, quick to complain of any breach of diplomatic etiquette or of the accepted rules of war. But the date of their victory over the Roman army, July 18, 390 B.C., is probably accurate, for it was kept ever after as a day of mourning in Rome.

So many Romans had been killed that the city could not be defended. A few young warriors decided to hold the Capitol, the flat-topped citadel on which stood the most sacred temples. The women and children, carrying the Sacred Things, fled across the Tiber to Etruria. Those senators and magistrates who were too old either to fight or to flee sat on their ivory thrones in the Forum, awaiting death. Brennus, the Gallic chieftain, led his horde into Rome.

After they had killed the senators and sacked the city, the Gauls besieged the Capitol. They nearly got in by escalade, but at the last minute Juno's sacred geese gave the alarm. This was clearly a reward for the piety of the Roman garrison, who, despite their hunger, had spared the sacred geese.

The final stages of the legend are most confused. Apparently Brennus agreed to take a ransom and leave the Capitol unharmed; then he cheated by producing false weights with which to weigh the gold; then an unexplained Roman army turned up to chase him away, leaving the ransom behind him.

It seems clear that the Gauls did indeed sack most of Rome, failed to take the Capitol, and then went back to the Po valley. If any records had been kept of earlier Roman history they were destroyed in this war, which explains why we must rely on legend.

The Romans set about restoring their dominion over central Italy, where their neighbors had also been weakened by Gallic raids. By the year 343 B.C. they had done so.

# THE PUNIC WARS

The Romans were a naturally conservative people, respectful of their betters. The Comitia made laws, and the tribunes protected the lower orders; but the day-to-day government of the city was in the hands of the Senate. The Senate met on every working day and held genuine debates, especially on foreign policy. Declarations of war and treaties of peace had to be ratified by the Comitia; but the Comitia met rarely and then voted after little discussion. Only the Senate could go into things thoroughly.

There was some difficulty in keeping up the numbers of the senators, as they dropped out through old age and death. In very early days the king had nominated new senators; under the Republic that became the duty of the consuls, who succeeded to most of the kingly power. But every consul, during his single year of office, was anxious to lead out the army and win a famous victory; choosing senators was an unimportant chore which was apt to be neglected.

Presently a new office was set up, the censorship. There were normally two censors, for the Romans always feared a single magistrate. Their chief duty was to assign each citizen his correct rank. Each Roman who could provide, out of his own purse, full armor with spear, shield, and sword was assigned to a voting unit of one hundred men, and that unit had one vote in the Comitia. Poorer citizens, down to the proletariat who could not buy weapons and were valuable only because they might produce citizen-children, were assigned to more numerous companies, also each with one vote. Knights, who could keep a horse, were put into units of less than a hundred. Most Greek cities had a similar arrangement, the man who turned out equipped for battle having a bigger vote than the unarmed pauper; but only the Romans carried it out so thoroughly. Everything they undertook they carried out thoroughly, and in their eyes the principal duty of a citizen was to fight for his city.

In the course of allotting proper places the censors also nominated new senators, and they were empowered to remove any senator for unbecoming conduct. Censors were elected every five years, but they were expected to complete their task and resign from office after two years.

When the censors reported to the Comitia they gave, among other things, the number of the army; and to number the army, which looks like boasting of your might, nearly always offends the gods. (This was a very ancient belief; you will remember that even King David of the Old Testament found it dangerous.) So the censors were always elderly, venerable men, skilled in the art of placating the gods. That they were elected by the Comitia is not surprising; the Comitia also elected the Pontifex Maximus, the chief priest of Jupiter, and all other important priests. The Romans recognized no distinction between religious and secular affairs.

Some figures of the census made by Appius Claudius in 312 B.C. show that by this time Rome had become a populous city. He decreed that even a landless man, a day laborer, might be a citizen, even though most of these poor workingmen were the descendants of freed slaves. Such proletarians would have little voting power; but the status of a citizen, with its right of appeal to the Comitia from the sentence of a magistrate, was valuable in itself.

The Romans were going ahead. Since the fifth century B.C. they had possessed a written code of law. That code could be understood by Cicero, whose language in turn we can read today; so that Latin, which can still be understood by a few learned men, has a continuous history of more than two thousand years.

Before those laws were published, there had been a brisk political struggle. Patricians, especially those who were priests, held that the laws were so intimately concerned with the gods that mere plebeians should not know them. Plebeians maintained that patrician wise men altered the unwritten laws to suit their personal convenience. In the end the laws were written on twelve tablets, and put up in the Forum for all to see.

At this time Roman law was still a series of primitive answers to questions: "If A has done X then B should be done to him." As a rule the penalty was fixed and the judges could not lessen it. But Romans did not like to sentence a fellow citizen to death; the convention grew up that in serious cases the court would adjourn until next morning before passing sentence. If the culprit took the hint and fled, sentence would never be pronounced. But lifelong exile was a fate only a little better than death, for to most Romans the political activities of the Forum were what gave meaning to life.

In Rome there were no professional lawyers. Every citizen was presumed to know the law, and to be capable of speaking for himself in any lawsuit. But a friend of his, more eloquent or more distinguished, might speak for him as a favor, without payment. In minor cases the judge was the praetor, a politician with no previous legal training who got through his cases by applying the law literally and clumsily; but anything important, especially anything with a political flavor, would be decided by a very numerous jury, perhaps more than a hundred strong. Such a big jury was practically a public meeting and, like most public meetings, was governed by its heart rather than its head. The courtroom speeches of Cicero which have come down to us consist almost entirely of vulgar abuse and appeals to prejudice, without any effort to prove what actually happened. Roman law did not become an efficient and flexible code until it had been edited by the later emperors and their trained civil servants.

The same Appius Claudius who had taken the census also built the first Roman road, still known as the Appian Way. Romans invented roads, entirely out of their own heads. Thousands of years earlier the Minoans of Crete had laid cobblestones on muddy patches of an existing path, for example on the way to Mycenae; archaeologists who find them today claim them as examples of early roads. But a true Roman road was a very different thing.

Roman engineers laid out a new road in a dead straight line from one skyline to the next. That is why a Roman road, when it changes direction at all, changes direction on top of a hill. Roman workmen dug ditches on either side, perhaps put in curbs to hold all together, than laid foundations as they would for a house. The paving stones on top are only the final touch to a considerable bed of masonry, layer after layer of crushed stone or cement. The Via Appia, built in the fourth century B.C., is still plainly to be seen. Roman roads were built for men to walk on, but our modern highways are built by essentially the same method.

Naturally, where Romans built a road Roman soldiers would march. The Via Appia brought Roman soldiers to the civilized south of Italy, where Greek colonists had founded independent cities. The Greeks of Tarentum in particular were annoyed by this intrusion; they themselves were not very fond of fighting, so they hired King Pyrrhus of Epirus, across the Adriatic, to drive away these foreigners.

Pyrrhus was a famous Greek general. He led an army of trained Greek mercenaries furnished with all the latest weapons, including elephants from India. Several times the Romans were driven from the field with heavy losses, but they quickly learned to cope with elephants by mounting stoves on chariots and throwing hot coals at them. The Romans never fled in panic, and they always killed a great many Greeks before retreating. In the end King Pyrrhus decided that his victories were costing him more lives than they were worth, from which we get the phrase "Pyrrhic victory." So he went off to fight the Carthaginians in Sicily. Without their hired expert the Tarentines were easily beaten.

This was the second great crisis of the Roman state (the first had been the Gallic invasion). Primitive little Rome, whose citizens still lived in square wooden huts and dressed in rough lengths of unbleached wool, had taken on the most up-to-date army in the world and beaten it. The Greeks were especially impressed by the public spirit and financial probity of the Romans. Cineas, the Greek politician whom King Pyrrhus dispatched to buy a favorable peace from the Senate, reported to his master that bribery was useless in Rome and that every man of the three hundred senators was worthy to be a king.

Curiously enough, though the Romans had come into contact with the most developed form of Greek civilization, so far Greek culture made no impression on them. In fact, it was about this time that they adopted the most barbarous of their customs.

The Etruscans, though they had not been very successful in managing their temporal affairs, had impressed on all their neighbors that they really did know how to please the gods and foretell the future. The Roman method of identifying good or bad luck by the flight of birds may have been of Etruscan origin, as was certainly the other common method, inspection of the liver of a sacrificed animal. Etruscans were also supposed to know a lot about conditions in the next world.

Like most Italians the Etruscans were literal-minded. At one time they had followed the custom of killing all the slaves of a dead noble, so that the slaves might continue to wait on their master's spirit after his death. To barbarians that must have seemed mere common sense, and the practice is found in many ancient communities. Later the Etruscans introduced a refinement. To kill all the slaves in a household was hard on the heir, so only certain slaves would be killed. Which slaves? Obviously the choice should be left to the gods. Let slaves fight one another in single combat, and then Mars the war god could choose the victim who pleased him. These fights were also fun to watch, provided you were not a slave.

The Romans copied this Etruscan religious practice, until it became their favorite amusement. An heir might buy strong fighting-slaves just to make a good show at his father's funeral, though that contradicted the whole meaning of the rite, which was that a man's own slaves should

follow him to the grave. Just when the rest of the civilized world was getting rid of the last vestiges of human sacrifice, the Romans adopted it on a huge scale.

They made men kill one another by the hundreds, for the pleasure of watching them die. Intelligent Romans tried to find excuses for the custom. They said it was enjoined by religion, which was true only in part, for it was enjoined by the Etruscan religion, not by the ancient religion of Rome. They said it taught the spectators to look unmoved on wounds and death, and that this was valuable military training, which they must have known to be nonsense—and anyway the old men and the women who made up a large proportion of the spectators were not in need of military training. The games of the amphitheater are the greatest blot on Roman culture. Contemporary Greeks, even contemporary barbarians, thought them revolting. Many Romans also knew that they were revolting; but they so much enjoyed watching the slaughter that they could not bring themselves to abolish it.

While the Romans were expanding into southern Italy, Sicily became the theater of a bitter war between Carthaginians and Greeks. Carthage was a city on the north coast of Africa, founded by Punic emigrants from Tyre and Sidon in ancient Phoenicia. They were daring seamen, who traded up the Atlantic coast of Spain and even as far as Britain, then considered to be the extreme edge of the inhabited world.

There were not very many of them, but they had plenty of money, and they ruled their possessions in Africa, Spain, and Sicily by hiring foreign mercenaries to fight under Carthaginian generals. In Sicily a band of these mercenaries revolted and seized the city of Messina. In origin they were stray cutthroats from Italy, and they called themselves the Mamertines, the children of Mars. In 264 B.C. they appealed to Rome, the leading Italian power, to protect them from Carthaginian vengeance. After some hesitation the Romans decided to send an army overseas to help these disreputable allies.

So began the great Punic Wars, which lasted on and off from 264 to 146 B.C., and ended with Rome the greatest power in all the lands bordering the Mediterranean. Looking back, later Romans saw this as the heroic age of their city, when patriotism overcame faction and everyone did his duty. Certainly the Romans fought with amazing gallantry.

They had to begin by building a fleet to ferry the army to Sicily. They knew nothing about the building of warships, but luckily a Carthaginian warship was wrecked on the coast of Latium and they used it as a model. Whole forests were cut down for ship timber, and ships were built by the hundreds. These ships must be moved by oars, and the Romans, who knew nothing of seafaring, needed smooth water to practice their rowing. As there were no large harbors on the western coast of Italy, the Romans dug a navigable channel between the sea and an inland lake where their crews might train. Such enormous public works, all done without the aid of machinery, were a Roman specialty; they were no more daunted by the size of the task ahead than was the Egyptian who laid the first block of what was to become the Great Pyramid.

Once the army was in Sicily, the Roman peasant-soldiers usually beat the mercenaries of the Carthaginians. But their amateur fleet could seldom compete at sea with veteran Carthaginian sailors, and always suffered heavily in bad weather. So the Romans installed boarding bridges on their ships and fought the enemy as though on land. After long years of war the businesslike Carthaginians cut their losses, evacuated Sicily, and made peace.

Presently a young Carthaginian soldier, who had been chosen by his army to govern Spain in succession to his father, started the war again without consulting his home government. Hannibal was the most daring general of antiquity, and he conceived the idea of leading his men from Spain, across the Pyrenees, through southern Gaul, across the Alps, and so into Italy. He brought elephants with him, which of course made the journey more difficult; but he accomplished it. Arriving in northern Italy, he smashed the Roman army sent to meet him and then marched south to gather reinforcements from the disloyal subjects of Rome.

But he had misconceived the situation. The subjects of Carthage, heavily taxed and exploited, would have been eager to fight against their rulers; the subject allies of Rome, whose main duty was to provide a contingent for the glorious Roman army, were content with their lot. Hannibal received no important reinforcements, and was never strong enough to lay siege to the city of Rome.

For fifteen years Hannibal remained in southern Italy, at the head of his army of Spanish and Gallic mercenaries. Again and again he defeated the Roman generals sent against him, until it became accepted Roman strategy to lurk near the Carthaginian army but never to fight a set battle. But meanwhile the war spread. A Roman army drove the Carthaginians from Spain, another army campaigned toward the head of the Adriatic, at last another army landed in Africa. Hannibal was summoned home to defend his own city. At Zama, outside Carthage, he was beaten at last by the Roman general Scipio. The Carthaginians sued for peace.

The Second Punic War ended in 201 B.C. and the Third did not begin until 149 B.C. During these fifty years the Romans, without being especially aggressive or quarrelsome, conquered most of the civilized world.

The famous cities of ancient Greece were in decline. Athens, Sparta, and Thebes were still independent, but in military affairs they hardly counted. The other lands around the Aegean were grouped into kingdoms, ruled by descendants of the generals of Alexander the Great; and some of their kings, jealous of the new power of Rome, had supported Carthage in the late war.

Macedonia was the first kingdom to be conquered by the Romans, and that led to a general protectorate over the little cities of Greece proper. Then the Greek king of Egypt, the weakest of these new kings, begged the Romans to defend him against his enemies. That led to intervention in Syria and Asia Minor—intervention that was always victorious.

But though the Roman army was invincible the Romans still thought of themselves as newcomers to civilization, not yet worthy to rule cultured Greeks. When a Roman army had won its war it usually went home. After long hesitation and more than one war, Macedonia was annexed. But the Romans took less tribute from it than the Macedonians had previously paid to their own kings; they also closed the lucrative mines of gold and silver because they did not feel themselves competent to manage them. The famous cities of

Greece remained formally free, for any Roman would have considered it indecent to give orders to the assembly of Athens or the ephors of Sparta. Egypt, Syria, and the little states of Asia Minor were still ruled by worthless Greek dynasties, whose kings offered bribes to the nearest Roman general in the intervals of poisoning their fathers or being poisoned by their sons.

Nevertheless, Rome must have her own way, and her orders were sometimes peremptory. When Popilius, the Roman envoy, delivered an ultimatum to King Antiochus of Syria, the king asked for time to consider it. With his envoy's staff Popilius drew a circle around the feet of the king and said he must yield, or declare war, before he stepped out of it. King Antiochus submitted.

In Spain, Rome ruled the few towns which Carthage had founded, but left the barbarian tribes of the interior to manage their own affairs. The Romans hated sea travel, and the only road to Spain ran through southern Gaul; though Roman soldiers used it constantly, for part of the way it passed through foreign territory. In short, though by this time Rome was by far the strongest power in the Mediterranean, and every king or tribal chief between the Caucasus and the Atlantic feared her, the actual Roman Empire did not extend far beyond Italy.

Rome could no longer remain cut off from the civilization of Greece. Greek politicians, bribe in hand, constantly visited the Senate, which managed foreign affairs; besides, there was a party of native Romans who were eager to become as Greek as they could.

This party was led by Publius Scipio, the boy wonder who had beaten Hannibal at Zama. At the age of seventeen he had saved his father's life in battle, at twenty-four he had

*The Onager*

commanded the army in Spain, at thirty he was elected consul, and by the time he was thirty-three he had conquered
Carthage. Obviously there was no holding him, and he
wanted to absorb Greek culture.

With his brother Lucius Scipio, who was unfortunately a
corrupt and incompetent politician, he kept open house in
Rome for Greek writers and philosophers. He learned to
speak and read Greek, and passed on the knowledge he
acquired. But the Greeks of those days were not only tutors,
they also had inquiring minds. They wanted to get to the

bottom of any strange state of affairs, especially a political state of affairs. These Greeks were fascinated by the queer Roman way of doing things, and tried to understand the Roman constitution.

Rome was not a monarchy. Every Roman remembered how the kings had been driven out. Then, they reasoned, it must be either an oligarchy or a democracy, but which? The Senate did nearly everything, and was nearly always in session. Only on rare occasions did the people meet in Comitia to elect the more important magistrates. As a rule they elected candidates recommended by the Senate, but there was no law that they must do so. Anyone who inquired closely must decide that Rome was a democracy, in which the oligarchs of the Senate were encroaching on the rights of the people.

That became the opinion of Publius Scipio, but he failed as a leader of the people because he also thought of himself personally as so great that he was above the law. After a campaign in the east, his brother Lucius Scipio, accused of peculation, was commanded to produce his accounts. In open court Publius tore them up, saying that the Scipios, who had added so much to the wealth of Rome, should not be harried over trifles. So Publius himself was put on trial. He refused to defend himself; instead he pointed out that this was the anniversary of the battle of Zama and suggested that magistrates, jury, and spectators should accompany him to the temple of Mars to give thanks for that famous victory. Since everyone followed him the court stood adjourned, and the trial was never resumed.

Perhaps Scipio could have made himself king of Rome, but he did not want to. When he found that his colleagues in the Senate disliked him for his radical opinions he left Rome, and presently died on his country estate.

In appearance Rome was still an old-fashioned Italian town, even though its inhabitants were discussing Greek ideas. The large, square town houses of the rich were built of brick and wood, without stone, and they still centered around the smoky atrium. The only images of the gods were of painted terra cotta; the only ornaments of the temples were the painted terra cotta uprights called antefixes which closed the gap where the tiles of the roof met the wall. The Romans used mean furniture and dressed meanly, though senators had just begun to mark themselves off from the common herd by a purple stripe on the toga. Already some epics and plays were being written in Latin, by native Italians, though they followed Greek models as closely as they could. There were no splendid marble theaters as in Greece. When these plays were staged, as part of some religious festival, they were shown in temporary wooden booths.

In politics there had been two more or less accidental, unplanned developments. It was now very rare for anyone to reach the Senate unless he had a senator among his ancestors. A nobility was arising, of mixed patrician and plebeian stock; often the plebeian houses were the more conscious of their high birth. The second change was that the army was becoming divorced from the Comitia. Roman citizens were now numbered by the hundred thousands, many of them settled in the towns of Italy and rarely visiting Rome. There were so many of them that they were scarcely affected by conscription, and only a minority served in the army. But the contingents of Italian subject allies had not been reduced, though the native populations of these cities were declining. Most soldiers were no longer Romans, most Romans were no longer soldiers.

The right to vote in the Comitia was the least important of the privileges of citizenship. The voting units had been so gerrymandered that a personal vote had lost significance. But the legal immunities were valued. A citizen found guilty by a magistrate had the right of appeal to the Comitia. In practice a citizen was never condemned to death. It was easy to persuade the Comitia that an insult to any citizen was an insult to Rome; therefore no Greek king, and few Italian town councils, would dare to flog or imprison a Roman.

In the old days citizenship had been freely granted. Now that it was more valuable it was harder to get. Italians found to their annoyance that an honorable discharge from the army after long service did not carry with it the citizenship, as it used to do. They began to feel that they had been cheated.

In the year 149 B.C. the Romans fell into a hysterical panic at the quite imaginary menace of a revengeful Carthage. In 146, after a bitter siege, the inoffensive trading city was utterly destroyed, so that salt might be sown on its ruins in token that it remain desert forever. In the same year Corinth, the greatest commercial city in Greece, was destroyed as punishment for rebellion. The Romans were hitting out at imaginary dangers, which suggests that the Senate was losing its nerve.

# ROME THE MIGHTY

The Senate was indeed finding Rome a difficult city to govern. Great wealth flowing in from the new provinces demoralized the upper classes, and at the same time the populace was changing in character. By the old theory of the constitution the citizen who voted in Comitia was an independent yeoman farmer or a self-employed craftsman, who had served through two or three campaigns and would be called up for the army again if he voted for war; he had an interest in electing competent magistrates to command him in the field, and since he owed no man anything his judgment would be unfettered. Those were in fact the kind of men who had beaten Hannibal, but by now the picture was out of date.

Now the city was flooded with unemployed veterans. It had long been the practice to grant a free farm to a veteran, instead of a pension in money. After a victorious campaign there was plenty of unoccupied land, the spoils of war; and presumably the soldier had farmed before he was drafted. But after years of fighting among luxurious Greek cities, few veterans wished to go back to the plow tail. Most of them sold their land as soon as they were given it, and drifted to Rome to live in idleness.

There was a brisk market in land, another novelty. Italy is not well suited to wheat-growing, and from north Africa and Egypt wheat could be imported by sea to be sold more cheaply than the homegrown product. But in the days before refrigeration meat must be produced near its market; besides needing beef and mutton for the table the Romans consumed a great deal of wool in their togas, and an enormous quantity of leather, which they used instead of canvas for military tents.

Speculators bought up numbers of small arable farms and threw them together into extensive ranches, where sheep and cattle grazed under the care of a few herdsmen, usually barbarian slaves. Not only did the ex-soldiers prefer city life; there was no longer room for so many plowmen on the land.

In Rome the idle citizen could live on very little money, because of the development of the client system. In the beginning the head of a clan had looked after his poorer kinsmen; in particular he spoke for them in the law courts, where a respected noble, probably an ex-magistrate, would be heard with greater attention than a humble laborer. Now every rich man set himself up as a patron, the protector of as many clients as he could collect.

Probably the rich man had gained his wealth by unsalaried service to the state. The provinces, the overseas dominions of Rome, were no longer ruled by praetors elected annually for the purpose, as once Sicily and Sardinia had been ruled. There were just not enough suitable candidates for election. Instead, a praetor or consul was given a province at the end of his year of office in Rome, and governed it with the title of propraetor or proconsul. But the Greeks were accustomed to bribing their rulers, and at the end of his appointment the ex-magistrate would come home rich.

The more clients he could collect, the easier he would find it to keep his wealth.

The patron still spoke for his clients in the law courts, but now there was far more in the relationship. Every morning the clients called on their patron, who gave them a handout, in the form of either a meal or a small sum of money. Then, surrounded by his clients, the patron strolled down to the Forum. These dependents were something between a group of yes men and a bodyguard, and the bigger the crowd of clients the more important was the patron. But what really mattered was that in Comitia all these clients voted as their patron directed.

At a normal meeting of the Comitia only clients voted. Farmers and businessmen working hard all over Italy could not find time to visit Rome to vote in person for every official and magistrate. Thus, wealthy senators came to control the annual elections, and a convention grew up that only the sons of senators should seek office. By a complicated system of logrolling, the various senatorial families shared the plums of office. The central government was not very efficient; but three hundred senators, each jealous of all the others, saw to it that there was no danger of tyranny by one famous and popular man. The system worked fairly well, though earnest students of Greek political theory knew that it was not at all what they meant by democracy.

At the same time, the dominions of Rome continued to expand. This was partly because provincial governors had a very strong incentive to win a war of conquest. A general who had added to the wealth of Rome was entitled to a triumph, a splendid ceremony in which he led his army in procession through the city to the great temple of Jupiter on the Capitol. The victorious general wore a special dress and

rode in a special chariot. The spoils he had won were displayed in the procession. So were a few chosen prisoners, who were executed outside the temple at the moment the general sacrificed an ox; the general public might regard this as a just vengeance on the enemies of Rome, or as a human sacrifice, according to individual taste. A triumph must be decreed by a special vote of the Senate. The general who had been granted one was known for the rest of his life as

"triumphator," and wore "triumphal ornaments" on his toga. These ornaments, displayed on his image after he was dead, would reflect luster on his family to all eternity. It was the highest ambition of every Roman soldier to be granted a triumph, and many provincial governors would provoke a war against a weak neighbor in the hope of earning one.

The proconsul or propraetor in charge of a province had a very free hand. His chief duty was to command the garrison of Roman troops allotted to him by a decree of the Senate, but defense and the maintenance of order were only part of his responsibility. He was also supreme judge in all cases concerning provincials, though Roman citizens could appeal from him to the Comitia. The total tribute of his province had been fixed by law, but he apportioned this total among his various districts. If the provincials wanted to do anything out of the ordinary—build a bridge, drain a swamp, repair the walls of a city—they must first ask his permission. He might execute any of his subjects on a charge of disloyalty, or confiscate all his property.

The man who wielded these enormous powers came out for a single year to a foreign land, of whose language he was often ignorant. He had no training in the local laws or customs. There was no staff of professional civil servants to help him. His clerks would be his own slaves, bought with his own money; his personal friends might gain experience in administration by giving him a hand. He might get a small allowance for traveling expenses, but in general he drew no salary. After a year in office he expected to come home wealthy.

The governor did not collect the revenue. That was managed by an even more absurd system. Every year the total tribute of a province was sold by auction in Rome. The highest bidder paid over the price in advance, and then tried to increase his profit by collecting the taxes as cheaply and ruthlessly as possible. Such speculators were known as publicans; in the Gospels they are all assumed to be scoundrels.

During this period, the second century B.C., Roman rule over a foreign province brought peace; there was no danger from invasion, very little danger from bandits. But the Roman governor and his group of assistants were themselves remorseless plunderers, hated and feared by their subjects. Yet the provincials must obey, for the Roman army was invincible.

# BREAKDOWN OF THE CONSTITUTION

Publius Scipio, the student of Greek political theory who had been so famous that he could defy the law, died in retirement. His only child was a daughter, Cornelia, married to a senator named Gracchus. Gracchus died young, and Cornelia brought up her two sons according to the Greek theories of her father. When the elder, Tiberius Gracchus, was elected tribune in 133 B.C., he tried to introduce Greek democracy to Rome.

Now, the Roman constitution could work only so long as no one thought about it too carefully. In strict legal theory there were a thousand opportunities to stop anything from being done at all. One consul could countermand all the orders of the other equal consul; one of the ten tribunes might veto any particular proposal, though no one had decided what would happen if another tribune vetoed the first veto; various priests and augurs could adjourn a political gathering, or indeed a projected attack on a hostile army, by announcing that the gods were angry and that it would be wiser to wait until they were in a good temper.

In fact the Romans took decisions and carried them out, because the various magistrates worked together. They all knew that they would go out of office at the end of the year, and that then it would be their turn to be governed by others; common prudence, as well as justice, forbade them to harry personal enemies who might soon be their rulers. Tiberius Gracchus was made of sterner stuff.

His quarrel with the Senate was ostensibly about the distribution of public land, an explosive topic at the best of times. But underneath lay a deeper issue. If Rome was a democracy, said Gracchus, then the people assembled in Comitia could vote to alter the ancestral constitution. The Senate maintained that the ancestral constitution was sacred and unalterable. It is an issue which is still unsolved.

Gracchus never noticed that the Comitia, filled with city idlers, no longer represented the people of Rome. When he pushed his argument until it came to the sword, the people showed that they were not behind him. The senators, coming down to the Forum armed with clubs, killed Gracchus and some hundreds of his adherents. A few years later they killed his brother Gaius, who tried to revive the quarrel.

For the first time in its long history there had been fighting within the walls of Rome. The great civil war had begun. It lasted on and off, with intervals of truce rather than peace, from 133 B.C. until the Empire was set up in 27 B.C. In its early stages it was complicated by another concurrent civil war, in which the Italians who made up most of the Roman army fought savagely to be granted full citizenship. Though the Italians lost this war they won the peace. In the end the citizenship was extended to practically every free man who could speak Latin, and the Italians returned to being loyal allies.

The party which wanted the Senate to remain the governing body of Rome called themselves the "Optimates," the men of good birth. They were also, we must remember, the party which upheld personal liberty. They wanted the government to be weak, so that every citizen should be free— free not only in his political opinions but in his private life. They favored peace and a small empire, because war gave too much power to a victorious general, and the rule of more provinces would enlarge the governing circle. But though the Senate as a whole favored peace, each individual senator would like to earn a triumph; as soon as he got command of an army he tried to provoke a war of conquest.

The other party, which wanted to make the Comitia the governing body, called themselves the "Populars." They wished to see a strong government ordering citizens about in the name of the people. They knew that an assembly of all the citizens of Rome could not manage the day-to-day administration of the state, and no one had yet hit on the idea of parliamentary representation; they wanted to choose one leader and give him unlimited power. So long as the majority of the people supported him, they would have the equivalent of popular government.

During these long wars there were other changes. Marius, one of the Popular tyrants, reorganized the Roman army to make it into the professional force which ruled the civilized world for the next three hundred years.

Allies and subjects provided cavalry and skirmishers; every Roman soldier was an infantryman of the line. The basic unit was the legion of 6,000 men, divided into ten cohorts and sixty centuries. Each cohort was commanded by a military tribune, a commissioned officer chosen by the Comitia; the legion was commanded by a legate, a nobleman appointed by the commander in chief. These were the only commissioned officers; each century was led by a centurion risen from the ranks, with lesser noncommissioned officers to help him. The centuries were numbered and centurions were promoted to the lower numbers; the centurion of the first century, known as *primipilus* or first javelin, was the senior noncommissioned officer of a body equivalent to a modern division, and a very great man indeed.

The draft had been abolished. Every legionary was a volunteer and, in theory, a full Roman citizen. He enlisted for at least sixteen years and as a recruit was carefully trained. All centurions carried, and used, stout cudgels to keep their men in line. But though the legionary lived under strict discipline he was well paid and well fed. At the end of his service he expected a good farm or its value in money, and was likely to start a civil war if his general did not get it for him. A soldier was a man of substance, who expected to live without working after he had retired.

What gave him importance was his thorough training. A cohort of trained soldiers used their weapons so skillfully that no number of untrained civilians could stand against them. If an army was suddenly needed in some emergency or civil war, it was wiser to call up retired veterans than to embody civilian recruits.

Marius, an organizer of genius, devised all the equipment of the Roman army. A legionary was the only soldier of that period who did not carry a long spear. Greeks fought in the phalanx, a dense column of pikemen; among barbarians good metalwork was so rare that common tribesmen used long flimsy spears and only wealthy chiefs carried rapiers. Romans relied on the short broadsword, double-edged and with a sharp point. It was deadly in the hands of a skilled fencer, and nearly useless when wielded by an untrained novice.

Marius saw that if the army of one city was to conquer the civilized world each Roman soldier must be able to take on several opponents. Therefore he must fight as an individual, not jam himself against his neighbor like a Greek pikeman. A Roman legion was normally drawn up in three lines, each of three ranks, but with considerable intervals between the cohorts. Each man took post at arm's length from his neighbor. Thus, a legion of 6,000 men could overlap a Greek phalanx 16,000 strong.

A Roman soldier carried an oblong leather shield with a metal boss; it was large enough to protect him from neck to knee. In his left hand were two metal-tipped javelins, which he threw at close range just before the moment of impact. (Untrained men always threw them too soon, to have time to draw their swords.) On his head was a stout helmet, but his leather cuirass was flimsy. His thighs were protected by stout leather straps dangling from the cuirass, but his buttocks were covered only by the kilt-like tail of his tunic. For ease in marching his legs were bare, save for ankle-high military boots. To Romans, who normally wore light sandals or went barefoot, these boots were characteristic of military dress, so that a man in uniform was said to be "booted."

Roman soldiers were trained to march as thoroughly as they were trained to fight. Every legion was expected to cover twenty miles a day, day after day, and to build a fortified camp every evening, even if it were to be occupied only for one night. Especially in Scotland, which was traversed but not garrisoned by Roman armies, these temporary Roman camps can still be seen on the ground. Like everything else planned by a Roman mind, the camp would be square; it was guarded by a deep ditch with a rampart behind, and on the crest of the rampart was a line of stakes. Next day each soldier would carry off two stakes, to save time in making that evening's camp. Within, the camp was divided by wide streets into square blocks of huts. Headquarters and stores were always in the same part of the camp, as were the huts of each cohort; every man could find his place and begin building without waiting for special instructions.

A mule train followed the legion; but the mules had to carry nothing but sacks of grain for the men's porridge, and skins of wine which was mixed with great quantities of water for their drink. These Roman heavy infantry were as mobile as light-armed raiders. They could outmarch any Greek army, which was encumbered with tents and ox carts. Some barbarians might move faster, but they carried no supplies and began to starve if they could not plunder every day. The Roman armies that fought the great civil war were the most efficient military machines that existed before the days of gunpowder.

These Roman soldiers knew themselves to be something special. They despised the old men of the Senate and the idlers of the Comitia, in theory the authority which commanded their commanders. Furthermore, Marius had introduced the dangerous innovation that recruits should swear obedience to him personally, not to the city of Rome; naturally, other commanders followed his example.

At first the danger was concealed, because both the people of Rome and the army were wholehearted supporters of Marius. He was elected to four consulships in a row, though he had started life as a landless laborer and was not by birth the kind of man who normally held office. For the first time in recorded history a German army invaded Gaul and threatened Italy. Marius destroyed it, and after that nothing was too good for him.

Then a rebellion broke out in the city of Rome. After

some hesitation Marius suppressed it, which was his duty as consul. But his supporters now despised him as a turncoat, and the Optimates distrusted him because he had hesitated before choosing his side. Marius went off to tour the holy shrines of Asia, because he dared not live as a private citizen in the city he had lately ruled.

That was a terrible portent. Hitherto the most eminent consuls had safely retired into private life after holding office. But party strife was growing dangerous. Before Marius could come back the Italians rebelled, and the command of the Roman army was given to a young noble named Sulla. In 88 B.C., more than forty years after Gracchus had begun the civil war, Sulla lost the extremely riotous consular elections. He did not retire into private life, he did not even go abroad until things had blown over; instead he led his faithful army straight against the city of Rome, and captured it as though it had been an enemy fortress.

Soon Sulla went east to fight against Mithridates, king of Pontus, who had raised all Asia Minor against Rome, massacred 80,000 Italians who lived overseas, and advanced as far as Athens. So while Sulla was defeating Mithridates, Marius reoccupied Rome at the head of an army of brigands and freed slaves.

Marius died soon after, during his seventh consulship; no man before him had been consul more than twice. Then Sulla came home with his army, and recaptured Rome from the Populars. He set the Optimates so firmly in power that he was able to die peacefully in his bed, after retiring from office; but as soon as he was dead, in 78 B.C., the city was troubled by Popular revolts.

These civil wars were terribly destructive of Roman lives, and not only on the battlefield. As each side in turn gained

control of the machinery of government, it set about exter-
minating the leaders of its enemies by the method of proscrip-
tion, which is Latin for writing up a list. A list of the names
of those condemned was posted up in the Forum. There had
been no accusation and no trial; often the first that the victim knew of his danger was when he read his own name in
the Forum, which every Roman politician visited every day.
The man proscribed was killed immediately, and all his
property confiscated by the ruling party; though if he tried
to escape, the man who caught him got some share of it as a
reward.

The system was devised to kill promising young men, who
were just beginning to be known; its effect in lowering the
standard of Roman intelligence cannot be calculated.
Luckily the damage was slightly mitigated by that other
great Roman institution, family influence. Sulla very nearly
proscribed young Julius Caesar, for the Caesars were notori-
ous Populars for all their high descent. But Caesar's rela-
tives on his mother's side, the Cottas, were equally eminent
Optimates, and they combined to beg Caesar off; nevertheless
young Caesar thought it prudent to go into hiding for a time.

A young man of good family could not opt out of the
struggle and stay neutral. It was taken for granted that every
young nobleman was eager for office, and his only chance of
continued existence was to keep his side in power or to flee
before the executioner caught him. The struggle wasted
promising lives, though there was usually a rebellious
province somewhere which could offer shelter to the Outs,
as Spain under Sertorius gave shelter to hunted Populars.

With all this property being confiscated there were great
opportunities for the daring to grow rich. But the land they
bought—for land seemed the only safe investment—was ex-

*Julius
Caesar*

ploited as thoroughly and quickly as possible, so that the owner might make a profit before the other side took it back. The result was an increase in ranching by slave herdsmen, and less land than ever before for honest Italian plowmen. At the same time, since wealth might vanish so suddenly, there was an increase in ostentation. Slave retinues increased in the great houses, and so did the slaughter of slave swordsmen in the games. Special prisons were set up where slaves might be taught to fight, behind locked doors.

In 73 B.C. the inmates of a slave fencing school in Capua carried out a successful mutiny. They were all trained swordsmen, and their leader, a Thracian named Spartacus, was a soldier of great ability. After capturing the city of Capua they overran all Campania. In an effort to make civil war more difficult, Sulla had removed all regular Roman troops from Italy; the nearest legions were on the Po, in Cisalpine Gaul. Slaves from the great ranches flocked to join the gladiators. By the end of the year 72 B.C. Spartacus, now at the head of 100,000 men, had defeated both consuls and was threatening to march on Rome.

But in 71 B.C. Crassus, a noble though he was the richest businessman in Rome, as praetor took command of the

troops from Cisalpine Gaul and defeated the gladiators. Most of the slaves were killed in battle, but enough were taken alive to provide a continuous line of crucified figures writhing beside the road from Capua all the way to Rome.

Crassus was an eccentric, the only noble Roman of this period who liked to make money in business, instead of taking it from his enemies by force. In those days there were absolutely no public services in the huge city of Rome, so Crassus organized a private band of slave firemen. When a house caught fire he would offer to buy the burning building. If the price was right he bought it and his slaves put out the fire; if it wasn't, they didn't.

Crassus won fame by his victory over Spartacus, but other would-be leaders must make themselves known by foreign conquest. Pompey—a great soldier who began as an Optimate, switched to the Populars, and then finished as an Optimate again—brought under Roman rule Armenia and Syria and Palestine, indeed all the East as far as the Caucasus. His younger rival, Caesar, conquered Gaul and invaded Britain for no better reason than to win the devotion of his soldiers and to make himself known to the voters at home. So long as Crassus lived he made a third in the government and thus prevented a deadly duel; but Crassus went off to fight the Parthians on the far side of Syria, and was killed with most of his army.

Then Caesar and Pompey fought it out all over the Mediterranean world, in Greece and Egypt and Africa and Spain. When Caesar had won he was sole master of Rome. As leader of the Populars he was by political theory endowed with all the power of the sovereign people. His recommendation was enough to appoint a consul or pass a law. Elections remained as a form, for the Romans were scrupulous to observe ancient forms, but they were no longer contested.

Soon after he had won this round of the civil war, Caesar was murdered in the Senate House. His murderers were a group of senators, mostly members of his own Popular faction; they wanted him out of the way because his greatness blocked promotion. Caesar left no male heirs. His power passed to his second in command, Mark Antony, until Caesar's nearest surviving male kinsman, his great-nephew Octavius, also claimed it. The civil war began again, first directed against the murderers of Caesar, then as internal strife within the Popular party. By the year 27 B.C. Octavius was supreme, so powerful that at the request of the Senate he took the surname of Augustus. He was still a young man; he had commanded armies when he was still below voting age. With his accession to power the great civil war, begun in 133 B.C. with the killing of Tiberius Gracchus, was finally at an end. The Populars had won, and as might have been foreseen the fruit of their victory was tyranny. Augustus ruled for more than forty years, until 14 A.D., and he is generally reckoned as the first of the Roman emperors.

# LIFE DURING
# THE GLORY OF ROME

We know more about the daily life of Rome in the first century B.C. than at any other period. It is considered to be the golden age of the Latin language, which altered from generation to generation like any other tongue; but though popular speech might change, educated men have tried to write in the style of the first century B.C. from that day to this. Furthermore, a great many prominent men of the period either wrote for publication, or at least carefully composed letters which were meant to be preserved by their recipients. Writings of that golden age were treasured in the Middle Ages as examples of good Latin, and are widely available now.

Before printing had been invented, how did these ancient Romans write for publication? Casual notes were scratched on wax-coated boards known as tablets, which could be folded together and tied with thread which was knotted and sealed for privacy; the letters were made with a blunt iron skewer known as a stylus, carried by every educated man as we carry fountain pens. When the murderers closed around Caesar he defended himself with his stylus. But for anything more than brief notes, the Romans wrote with reed pens dipped in ink, on paper made from the Egyptian papyrus plant. They wrote in our modern letters; or rather, we use the ancient Roman alphabet, a development of the earlier Greek alphabet.

Paper was made in rolls, say 10 inches wide by 10 feet long. The author wrote in vertical columns, from left to right. At each end of the roll was a stick, around which the paper was wound with the beginning on the outside; as the book was read it was wound around the stick at the left, until at the end of the reading, the book was inside out and must be wound back again. Paper made from papyrus was brittle and easily torn, and since there were no numbered pages it was hard to pick out a reference. Ancient authors usually quoted their authorities slightly inaccurately, from memory, because they were reluctant to handle their precious and fragile books.

A roll of this kind was known in Latin as a volume. One volume did not contain a great deal of writing and several were needed for most literary works. Nowadays *volume* is often translated "book," so that Caesar's *Gallic War* or Livy's *History* or any other ancient work is made up of many books.

Although all books were written by hand, in Rome they were fairly plentiful. Because of their numerous slaves the Romans were not interested in labor-saving machinery, but they took kindly to mass production. Professional book producers would buy the only copy of a new work from the author, and then have it read aloud to as many as a hundred copyists at once. In a few days an edition of several hundred copies could be produced. Unfortunately the slave-copyists were not very interested in their work, and if they misheard a passage were quite willing to write nonsense; scholars of the present day are still sometimes puzzled by it.

In ancient Rome it was possible, though not easy, to make a living by writing books. The publishers paid very little, but if an author became famous some rich man would be proud to set him up in a country estate; the author would repay his patron by dedicating further books to him.

Wealthy Romans did not read a great deal, though of course they could read easily. It was more usual to listen while an educated slave read aloud. Often, reading aloud was the chief entertainment at a party. An author would advertise his new work by reading it aloud to an invited audience.

Cicero, the greatest orator of his day and a prominent though unsuccessful politician, set the standard for Latin prose which still exists. He was a contemporary of Caesar, and was eventually murdered by Mark Antony. Among his works are the speeches he made in the law courts and various efforts to fit Greek philosophy into Latin dress. He was not a profound thinker, but he could express very gracefully the thought of others. He also left masses of private letters, which may or may not have been polished for publication. From them we get a clear picture of Roman life toward the end of the great civil war.

Though he was a self-made man, Cicero was not very interested in money. He could not charge a fee for defending a politician in the law courts, for in theory he was the patron and the accused was his client. If the client were acquitted he would give his patron a substantial present, and elderly admirers of eloquence left Cicero handsome legacies when they died. For one year he was consul, of course without a salary; the governorship of Cilicia which followed, though also unpaid, probably increased his fortune. Various people subscribed to keep him in comfort so that he could devote himself to politics on the Optimate side. He bought a number of country estates, though rather as pleasant places to live in than as productive investments. By modern standards his married life was odd. After many years of happy partnership he divorced his wife so as to marry an heiress much younger than himself. He was not ashamed of his conduct, and no one thought the worse of him for it.

His main interests were literature and politics. But to Cicero and his circle literature was very much of a game; it hardly mattered what you wrote, so long as you wrote it gracefully. A man who would write well could write on any subject. Cicero was quite willing to undertake a description of Britain, which he had never seen, if his brother, who had been there with Caesar's brief invasion, would send him a few notes about the island.

Politics was more important; Cicero knew that his head, and the heads of all his friends, was in danger. While in office, as consul or as governor of Cilicia, he had to work hard and make important decisions. But these appointments lasted only for a year; during other years politics consisted of endless personal gossip about which job should go to which man. Great issues were in dispute, for which great armies fought great battles; but these hardly appear in the petty tattle about Ins and Outs which fills Cicero's letters.

Cicero was essentially a civilized man, who would fit into any modern drawing room. His attitude to the gladiatorial games and to slavery, the atrocities of Roman life which shock us at the present day, is characteristic. Evidently the games sickened him, though he could not bring himself to say so; for they were a part of ancestral Rome, to be supported by all patriotic Romans. So he took the line that they were crude and boring, not horrible. As consul it was his duty to preside in the amphitheater, but instead of watching men die he went through his correspondence and dictated answers to his slave-secretary. He was proud that he had been there from start to finish like an ancient Roman, but glad that he had been too busy to see anything.

His attitude to the slaves he mentions in his letters was kindly. We must remember that there was no difference of race, very often no difference of language, between a Roman and his slaves. While the civil wars raged any harmless provincial, of any social class, might be reduced to slavery through no fault of his own (though a genuine Roman would instead die fighting). Presumably Cicero's estates were tilled by barbarian captives, who might be bought and sold, flogged or slain in the amphitheater, like so many dumb beasts; no Roman was interested, except financially, in their fate. But in his library and his office Cicero was served by educated Greeks, men of his own kind who became his collaborators and friends. Once he halted on a journey because his slave-secretary was too sick to travel, and when he had to go on, wrote careful directions for the nursing of the invalid. Most of his educated slaves were freed in middle age as a reward for good service; that was the general Roman custom, so that freedmen became a substantial and prosperous portion of the middle class. At the end, when Antony's soldiers were hunting him down, Cicero's slave litter-bearers were faithful to him. On the whole, to be Cicero's slave was not such a bad fate. But he had the legal right to crucify any slave at his mere whim; and at any moment, without warning, his slaves might be bought or inherited by someone who would do it.

When Cicero was caught and killed he was trying to escape overseas, dressed in his toga; he was probably the only ex-consul in all the civil wars who did not buckle on his sword and fight back. He was not a typical Roman, though we know more about him than about any of his contemporaries.

Like every other educated Roman, Cicero reverenced Greece as the home of learning. Athens had become practically a university town, and Rhodes was also a center of higher education. But it was knowledge and wisdom that the Romans admired, rather than Greek mastery in the plastic arts. In Rome itself there was little beauty, though statues of eminent men, made as lifelike as possible, filled the Forum. Pompey had built a famous town house, adorned with the beaks of captured warships, but the city was too crowded to have room for many palaces.

In their country houses, called villas, wealthy Romans had more scope. Although no villas have survived, we have written descriptions and a few unreliable pictures in mosaic. There was no attempt at an imposing façade; the buildings grew piece by piece, mostly on the ground floor. There were cool north-facing rooms for summer, and rooms heated by flues for winter. Steam baths were a Roman specialty, perhaps a Roman invention. From a furnace, usually under one wing of the house, hot air circulated below the floors of various rooms, at varying temperatures. Thus central heating would be provided throughout, and in addition there would be one very hot room where the bather could sweat, with a cold bath nearby.

Roman furniture was light and portable: little tripod tables, couches on which diners reclined. Some of it was very costly, made of rare wood or figured marble, and embellished with antique bronze. Greek statues were admired,

but with little discrimination. When Mummius, the Roman
commander who destroyed Corinth in 146 B.C., sent home a
shipload of Corinthian works of art, he warned the ship-
master that if any statues were damaged they must be re-
placed by others of equal worth. He obviously did not
know that the treasures of the temples of Corinth were ir-
replaceable! A century later the Romans were telling this
story against themselves, thinking that they now knew better.
Cicero wrote to a friend in Greece asking for some statues;
they were intended to adorn his library and so must be
Muses, not Bacchantes which were more appropriate to a
dining room. But Cicero did not specify the artist, or the
material, or the size of the statues, or indeed whether they
should be antique or newly made to his order. He wanted
Greek statues, because the best statues came from Greece,
and to him any Greek statue was the equal of any other
Greek statue.

When the wealthy and powerful Roman nobles were not
actually commanding an army or governing a province, they
found it hard to get through the empty days. It was unthink-
able that they should make money in business, or do any
work other than fighting or governing. One way to pass the
time was in dining. A respectable dinner party might last
literally for twelve hours, from midday to midnight. There
would be long intervals between the courses, during which
the guests sipped watered wine while a slave read from a new
book or recited ancient poetry; perhaps the host would set a
literary or philosophical theme for discussion.

Not all wealthy Romans were respectable. At other dinner
parties there would be less water in the wine. Dancing girls
or gladiators would fill the intervals between the courses;
guests whose appetites flagged could slip out to the *vomi-*

*torium*, and after tickling their throats with feathers would be ready to begin eating again.

Ladies never reclined on couches; they sat upright on chairs. As a rule they did not attend dinner parties, though sometimes the wife of the host would invite the wives of the male guests to a simultaneous party in her private apartments. Roman ladies were treated with great respect. They might receive gentlemen in their boudoirs, and we know that some of them wielded considerable political power—unlike Greek ladies, who were always kept at home and never allowed to meet a strange male. Divorce was permitted without restriction or formality at the bare request of the husband; but since he must then return all his wife's dower, which was usually valuable, the average husband thought twice before doing it.

To us this may seem an empty mode of life, but to the Roman noble it was the summit of felicity. Rome ruled the world, and he was helping to rule Rome. Over the dinner table he might talk about it by the hour. At one time Cicero was ordered to keep out of Rome, on pain of being prosecuted for what he had done as a consul. He had plenty of money and he went sightseeing in Greece, which he regarded as the most beautiful and intellectually exciting country in the world. But nothing could compensate for the personal gossip of Rome which he was missing; forgetful of his dignity he begged abjectly to return, until presently permission was granted.

BRITANNIA

London
(Londinium)

GAUL

SPAIN

ITALIA

Rome

MEDITERRANEAN

Carthage

SICILY

(Mare Nostrum)

# THE ROMAN EMPIRE
## AT ITS GREATEST EXTENT

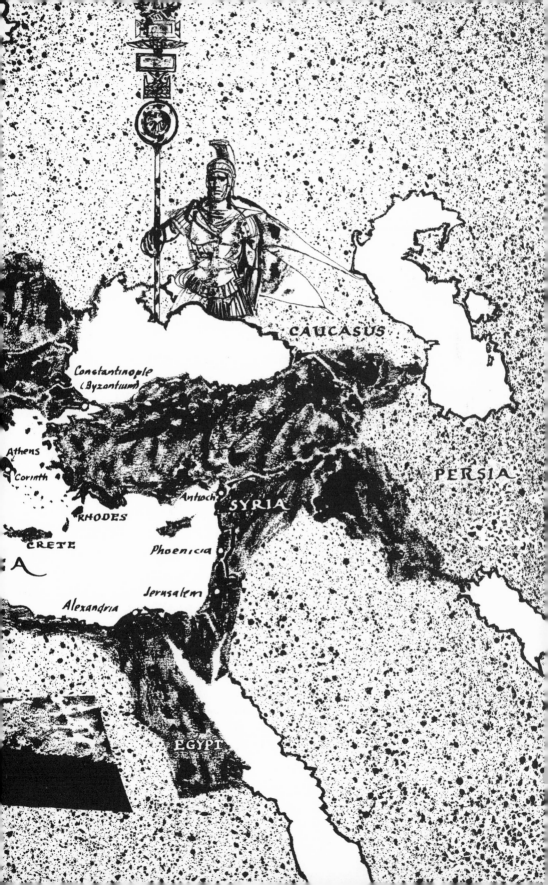

Constantinople
(Byzantium)

Athens

Corinth

RHODES

CRETE

A

Alexandria

Antioch

SYRIA

Phoenicia

Jerusalem

CAUCASUS

PERSIA

EGYPT

# THE EARLY EMPIRE

At first ordinary Romans did not notice Augustus had become an emperor. The title Imperator, held by many earlier soldiers, means no more than commander in chief. But Augustus commanded all the soldiers in the Roman army, and would command them until he died. His other offices were all known to the constitution, though never before had they been held in combination by one man for life. Consuls still presided in the Senate, where grave matters were solemnly discussed. But Augustus had nominated these consuls. As censor, Augustus could also appoint or dismiss senators at will.

The source of his power was the unswerving devotion of the army. Citizens could do nothing against trained legionaries, and every surviving legion had followed Augustus in civil war. If he wanted to get rid of an enemy he usually followed the forms of law, for no magistrate or jury dared to defy him. But if he was in a hurry he could tell any soldier to cut off the head of any citizen, and it would be done at once.

In daily life Augustus was a private citizen, though a very important one. In the Senate he always spoke first, so that the other senators should know what he wanted done; but he might not speak until the presiding consul had called on him. He lived in his private house, bought with his own money; it was a very large house, which covered most of the Palatine Hill and throughout the world the name palace came to designate the official residence of a ruler. The clerks who helped him to administer the Empire were his private slaves, or freedmen whom he himself had freed, for in Rome there was still no professional civil service.

This administration by slaves caused a great deal of bother. Roman citizens of good birth would not work as clerks for another Roman citizen; dignity forbade. But they resented taking orders from a minister who was or had been a slave.

The Senate also was a nuisance. Six hundred prominent and wealthy Roman noblemen wanted to do more than agree with everything Augustus proposed. They dared not disagree for fear of the soldiers, and anyway they were all Populars or they would not have sat in the Senate. They debated endlessly, trying to find a better way of doing what Augustus wanted done. He must sit in his place and listen patiently, or he would be accused of boorish disrespect for what was still in theory the supreme governing body of Rome. Furthermore, when the Senate tried to do anything it was maddeningly incompetent. Augustus would not allow senators to meddle with military affairs; but when he turned over to them the distribution of the grain supply of Rome and the upkeep of the roads he soon had to bring these matters back under the control of his own clerks to avoid chaos.

In the end Augustus ceased to attend the Senate. Instead, a few senators waited on him in his office, to give senatorial approval to whatever he had already decided. But until the end of the Empire relations between emperor and Senate were always bad; the senators were always taking offense at imperial neglect, and the busy emperor felt he was wasting his time when he talked to them.

Of course Augustus did not depend solely on military support. A large proportion of his subjects prospered under his rule and wished it to continue. These were the businessmen, whether citizens, provincials, or freed slaves. Rome itself was not an important mercantile center. Its poor lived on free grain, provided by the emperor; its rich were great landowners. There were few members of the middle class. But in all the provincial towns of Italy and the civilized East, merchants and craftsmen blessed the Empire which had brought peace. Their prosperity enabled them to pay the taxes which supported the soldiers, on whom all depended.

Augustus had indeed brought peace. One authority ruled from the Atlantic to the Caucasus, and during the forty years of his reign his only wars were against barbarians beyond the frontier. Taxes were light, for the government cost very little.

The various provinces of this great Empire had reached many different levels of development, but in general the most important division was that between the civilized East and the barbarian West.

Europe east of the Adriatic and south of the Danube, Asia Minor, and the Near East this side of the Euphrates had adopted Greek culture several centuries before in the days of Alexander the Great. All the fertile farm land of Egypt had been the private property of its Greek king, and after the death of Cleopatra became the private property of Augustus. Alexandria in Egypt and Antioch in Syria were modern but mighty cities, nearly as rich and populous as Rome. Athens and Sparta, small and poor but very famous, were still in theory independent allies of Rome, governed by their own citizens, though they had no armed forces. In general any Greek city was granted internal self-government; the local council could levy a tax for the repair of public buildings, and spend money on public amusements. St. Paul was proud to be a citizen of self-governing Tarsus, in Asia Minor.

Somewhere in the neighborhood would be a Roman garrison, its Roman commander appointed by the emperor. His main duty was to keep the peace and defend the frontier. He was paid by the emperor, and forbidden to pillage the provincials. In fact his main anxiety, as we learn from the letters of Pliny the Younger, a governor in the days of the Emperor Trajan, might be to stop his cities from falling into bankruptcy by trying to build more splendidly than his neighbors.

For the first time in history there were no pirates in the Mediterranean. Over all this great area there were no frontiers and no customs barriers, and through every land ran the good Roman roads. Egypt and north Africa sent grain to feed Rome; every province paid tribute. In general, the civilized East flourished under the Roman peace.

Gaul and Spain were beginning to emerge from barbarism. Augustus took an interest in their welfare, for they had been the scenes of famous exploits by his adoptive father Julius Caesar, and Gaul in particular had been loyal to him throughout the civil wars. Every Gallic tribe was recognized as a legal community and encouraged to build a real Roman town for its capital. Here in the West the Empire brought not only peace and order, it brought civilization as well. Within their walled towns, linked by good Roman roads, the barbarians were proud to be subjects of Rome. They soon began to speak Latin, from which developed modern French and Spanish.

At the center of the empire was the city of Rome, which flourished in a material sense. In old age Augustus boasted that he had found it built of brick and left it built of marble, which is as true as most such boasts if we remember that many of his buildings were really made of brick, under a thin facing of marble slabs.

At last there begins to be a true Roman art—though only the designer would be Roman, employing Greek craftsmen. The Romans needed a new kind of building, bigger than anything the Greeks had made before: law courts, amphitheaters, temples, aqueducts. They invented the formal open space, whereas the Greeks had never bothered about the sites of their great buildings; in ancient Athens the Parthenon could not be seen in its entirety, for it stood in a huddle of other sacred temples. A Roman temple was built on a high plinth (pedestal), in an open space, where all of it could be seen; and very often a triumphal roadway led to it through a line of balanced façades.

Roman architects employed two devices in particular, the arch and the dome. These were not new discoveries, as they had been known to the Greeks, who used them rarely.

Now aqueducts stretched across the country, long lines of arches bearing a stream of water from its source in the hills to a fountain in the town. It would have been easier to convey the water by pressure down a hill and up the other side of the valley to any point lower than its source. But the Romans could make watertight pipes only of expensive lead, since they had not discovered how to glaze earthenware. The water trickled gently within an open channel of brick and cement, supported on tremendous arches. These clumsy engineering devices were so soundly constructed that some of

them are still in use. Excellent construction was as typically
Roman as was clumsy design.

Domes were rather more difficult; they had to be made
first on a framework of wood, which afterward was taken
away. In the days of Augustus some mighty domes were
reared. As a Christian church the Pantheon still stands. Its
wide dome was made of Roman brick and mortar, which
have now set into one solid piece. One day perhaps it will fall
all together, still in one piece, but until then it will remain.

Of course the brick of this dome is hidden by thin slabs of
marble, inside and out. All the Pantheon looks like solid
marble, though there is brick underneath. But note that the
pillars of the porch, the steps, and the doorway are modeled
on the standard Greek work of the time, though on a bigger
scale than most Greek buildings. The Pantheon is a typical
Roman design of the early Empire.

Augustus looked after the poor of Rome. He gave them
free food, free amusements, and occasional gifts of money.
He built for them public baths, which were more like amusement parks than sanitary installations; within were playing
fields, libraries, restaurants, and bars, besides hot steam and
swimming pools. The poor, who mostly upheld the Popular
party, loved him.

The traders of the middle class also prospered under his
rule. Peace and good communications helped them to make
money, and the excellent Roman laws were now honestly
administered. All over Italy the little trading towns grew
rich.

But the nobility found themselves without an occupation.
Augustus, who was a bit of a snob, revered great nobles.
But he could not trust them to govern provinces, for fear of

rebellion; and in the Senate they could only support what the emperor had proposed. The fascinating political plotting which had been the main interest of their fathers was now forbidden, and those who still practiced it might be executed for treason.

As a result the nobles were always disloyal. They were very rich, but they despised business; they could spend their money only on feasting and luxury. They had great prestige, and many of them great intelligence; but they were not allowed to serve the state. Plotting became the only amusement of those too quick-witted to be satisfied with the formal honors of the consulship. Under Augustus they plotted to kill the emperor and bring back the Republic; under later emperors, when they saw that such a program was impossible, they plotted to kill the reigning monarch and set up one of themselves in his stead. Many plots were discovered, and a great many noblemen were executed for treason; nevertheless a great many emperors were murdered.

During the first century of our era, Roman citizens were a minority among the provincials. Though there was no more voting, the citizenship still carried valuable privileges. For example, under the Emperor Nero Saints Peter and Paul were both killed in Rome for the crime of being Christians. Now, St. Paul had been born a Roman citizen, though strictly speaking a Jew by religion should not have been granted the citizenship; presumably his father or grandfather had bought his rights from some Roman commander in Asia pressed for money during the civil wars. After his conviction in a public trial, St. Paul the citizen appealed to the emperor in person. Until the emperor had leisure to hear the appeal he was kept under house arrest in Rome, with sufficient personal liberty to be able to write most of his

Epistles. Finally, a soldier cut off his head with a sword, the most honorable and least painful method of execution. St. Peter the provincial, on the other hand, was just tortured to death as a nuisance, apparently without any form of trial.

In foreign policy Augustus stood for peace. There was only one civilized power on his border, Parthia beyond the Euphrates. But the Parthians were a conquering aristocracy, ruling a populace of disloyal Persians; they also wanted peace. A treaty was arranged, though to be on the safe side a large Roman garrison was stationed in Syria. Africa also had a small garrison, but the nomads of the Sahara were not dangerous.

In Europe the frontier of the empire was marked by the Rhine and the Danube; fortifications closed the gap between the headwaters of the two rivers. Beyond them lay bar-barians, with whom it was impossible to conclude treaties. Only strong Roman forces, raiding across the rivers into hostile country, could keep the foreigners at bay. On the Rhine was stationed the strongest Roman army in the Empire. The commanders of the two garrisons of Upper and Lower Germany were the most dangerous subjects of the emperor, capable of overthrowing him if they should combine in revolt.

At the beginning of his reign Augustus had led an enor-mous army, far more than his treasury could support, for by that time Roman soldiers expected high pay as well as a good bounty on discharge. Augustus disbanded all but twenty-five legions, whom he stationed permanently on the frontiers. A legion liked to stay in the same place, and some did not move for three hundred years. But it was a very small army to hold such a long frontier. There was no mobile field force. When the Emperor Claudius, who was the grandson of Livia the wife of Augustus, prepared to conquer Britain he had to collect troops from the garrisons of the Rhine; some legionaries protested at being removed from their ancestral home, though their camps were not more than fifty years old. One of the legions which conquered Britain remained in the island until the empire vanished.

Augustus decided that his dominions were as big as they should be and left written advice to his successors against further expansion. But he was dissatisfied with his German frontier. It required more men to hold the fortified lines, all the way up the Rhine to its source and then down the Danube to the Black Sea, than he could spare from his small army, yet the fierce barbarians of Upper Germany were still only a few days' march from the Alpine passes into Italy. If the frontier were advanced from the Rhine to the Elbe it would be very much shorter, and there would be plenty of friendly territory north of the Brenner Pass. For something like twenty years the Roman armies campaigned between these two rivers, until the eventual conquest seemed assured. Then in 9 A.D., when Augustus himself was too old to take the field, his general Varus and three whole legions were wiped out by the Germans. In despair, Augustus abandoned the war. The Rhine remained the Roman frontier.

The Roman armies were probably the best in the world at that time, but they were not quite invincible. Although Roman historians do not dwell on the subject, if you look carefully you will find that the Empire was repulsed from several projected conquests. Britain was subdued after a long war, marked by at least two resounding Roman disasters; and though Agricola marched through Scotland he did not conquer it. Agricola also thought of conquering Ireland, but his superiors would not even let him try. Numerous

Roman invasions north of the Danube left no lasting mark. In the East, Roman armies marched often to the Tigris, but the Euphrates remained the frontier. In the reign of Augustus the poet Horace celebrated the impending conquest of Arabia, but it never actually took place. Romans fought with confidence against any foe who met them, assembling a large army for a great battle; against guerrillas or light-armed skirmishers, in difficult country, they sometimes came off second best.

But what they had accomplished was an amazing achievement, and their self-confidence at that time is equally amazing. There were now a great many Roman citizens, but they were still a small minority of the population of the whole Mediterranean world. A citizen, even though he might have been born in Tarsus or Cadiz, usually thought of himself as a native of Rome. He would have ties of kinship and religion with some region of that city. Rome was one city, with one Capitol, one Forum, one Vestal hearth. Though it had outgrown its walls it had a definite boundary, so that a man might stand with one foot in Rome and the other outside it. Rome was a place, and in area not a very big place.

Yet Rome, this single city, ruled all the civilized world known to its inhabitants—from the Atlantic to the Caucasus, from the North Sea to the cataracts of the Nile. There were barbarians outside, lurking in the forests of Germany, wandering over the sands of the Sahara; but they were not worth bothering about. Rome did more than draw tribute from these many lands. In them every dispute was judged by Roman law, in a courthouse built according to the rules of Roman architecture, and the lawyers would plead in the Latin language. From Spain to Syria farmers might leave their cattle to graze in the open, secure under the protection

of Roman arms. Roman roads linked remote towns, all built
in the Roman style; harbors designed by Roman engineers
afforded safe shelter on every shore of the Mediterranean to
the cranky unseaworthy Roman ships. These hazardous
ships were at least in no danger from pirates; and though the
Romans never understood the sea they were as skillful in
navigation as any of their contemporaries.

In the poets of the Augustan age that glow of Roman
pride breathes through every line. When Augustus died in
his bed, a very old man, he had accomplished all that he set
out to do.

But he left some problems unsolved. His great task had
been to end the civil wars, and in pursuit of that aim he had
reduced the size of the army to a dangerous level. In the

cause of peace he had left the succession in doubt. It had never been decided whether in the future Rome should be ruled by an eternal line of emperors, or whether Augustus himself had restored the Republic after the tyrannies of the civil wars. Perhaps Augustus should not be blamed for that omission; it was a question which only the soldiers could decide.

The soldiers wanted another emperor; so the Senate appointed Tiberius, the stepson and heir of Augustus. Like his stepfather, Tiberius was a Julius by adoption, and thus the

hereditary leader of the Popular party. Luckily he was also one of the best generals of his day, who kept the Germans on their own side of the Rhine. Under his rule the Empire as a whole prospered, though from suspicion of possible rivals Tiberius persecuted the Roman nobility.

There followed three more emperors of the same family, descended from Livia, the wife of Augustus; of these Caligula was definitely mad, and Nero at least eccentric. But their connection with Augustus gave them the support of the soldiers and the Populars, until Nero went too far for even the most zealous partisan. He sang in public, and publicly recited poetry of his own composition. Perhaps he sang badly and his poetry was feeble, as reported by his detractors; but what really annoyed the Romans was that their emperor, who should have been fighting barbarians, instead took an interest in the arts. He had also murdered his mother, but that was not considered such a grave fault. When Nero learned that all his armies had rebelled against him, he killed himself.

The Romans were proud of their civilization; they liked convenient buildings, strong defenses, smooth roads. They also liked to watch magnificent processions and pageants in their theaters, though they no longer cared for Greek tragedy. But all these things ought to be provided for the warlike, ruling Romans by clever men who were their social inferiors. Every educated Roman was proud of his ability to write verse, but only for private recitation. He could judge a statue or a building, but it would never occur to him to make one. Every artist must work with his hands, and to work with your hands was disgraceful. To display your body in public was even more shameful. Nero was cruel; it was considered his greatest cruelty that he compelled respectable

Romans to perform in the theater. If he had merely sung to his friends at the supper table he might have been forgiven. But he sang his own songs on the public stage, and wore theatrical make-up.

Under such a Philistine system the arts declined, even though law and order protected the artist. But at the death of Nero even law and order, the characteristic Roman virtues, received a blow from which they did not recover. There were no more Julians, and the Empire became the prize of the most successful general. Never again did the Romans devise a method of succession other than civil war. The armies of Syria and the Rhine, which never left their permanent stations, very quickly developed corporate loyalties. An army which placed its general on the throne would be duly rewarded, an army beaten in the decisive battle would not be very sternly punished.

Besides, the soldiers were beginning to lose touch with civilian life. While Roman citizenship still mattered, every legionary had to be a Roman citizen. But only the infantry of the line were legionaries; all the cavalry, archers and slingers, scouts and other specialists, were recruited from the provinces, unless they were barbarian mercenaries from beyond the frontier. If these men survived to retire with a good discharge they would be granted citizenship. That made their sons citizens also, and so eligible for the legions.

Soldiering was very largely a hereditary occupation. Discharged soldiers settled on their bonus farms near the great fortresses, and sent their sons to serve on the same station. They must have married local girls, for no other girls were available. They had no reason to visit civilized Italy or Greece, no incentive to leave the frontier districts ruled by martial law, where a discharged soldier was somebody. Very soon, by 100 A.D. at the latest, the armies on the Rhine were composed of Gauls, the armies in Britain of Britons, those in Syria of Syrians.

From pride in their own trade and their own legions these soldiers beat back the barbarians from the frontier. But they felt no sympathy for the soft civilians of the interior provinces; and when they were ordered to march through Italy in the course of some civil war they gladly laid waste a country which seemed foreign to them. No contender for the throne dared to punish his men for plundering, since he depended on their willingness to fight for him. Civil war did immense damage.

Of course some emperors were able to transmit their power peacefully, especially if the heir was competent and about the right age. But an imperial dynasty seldom survived beyond the third generation. The conditions of court life were too great a handicap.

Here is an example: A middle-aged general fights his way to the throne. He is a good soldier who has come to the top by his own merit, for young men with great family influence were not welcome in the army. He rules with ability, though perhaps with severity, until he dies of old age and leaves the throne to his son. That son will be in the prime of life, and probably quite capable of holding down the job which has fallen into his lap; for he had an excellent private education while his father was still a general. But *his* son, who succeeds in his turn, is very soon overthrown by universal consent. He has been heir to the Empire since he was in his cradle; and unceasing flattery, coupled with absolute power to enjoy himself in any way he pleases, has unsettled his wits.

Every emperor was perpetually on the lookout for rivals;

so the other officials, who in theory shared some of his responsibility, feared to display any initiative. A consul or a senator who made a name for himself might be executed on bare suspicion, and even a provincial governor had better not be too good at his job. Thus, every sphere of government became the duty of the emperor, and if he chose to neglect it nothing at all was done.

Nevertheless the Roman Empire enjoyed one particular golden age, lasting for nearly a century. Between Nerva, who ascended the throne in 96 A.D., and Marcus Aurelius, who died in 180 A.D., all the emperors were able and virtuous. This was largely because they tried out a new principle of succession. The dying emperor left his dominions by will to the most promising of his generals. The new emperor declared himself to be the adopted son of his predecessor, for in Roman law adoption was a most solemn and binding ceremony. Thus, for more than eighty years there were no devastating civil wars.

But, until Marcus Aurelius, all these good Emperors who left their dominions to worthy strangers had no sons of their own. When at last the tie of blood came into conflict with the principle of adoption, family feeling won hands down. Marcus Aurelius insisted that his son Commodus should succeed him, though everyone except his father knew that Commodus was a worthless rascal. After twelve years of crime Commodus was murdered and the civil wars began all over again.

The memory of those eighty years of peace and prosperity remained with the Romans. That was what the Empire ought to be—what it would be as soon as the next good emperor took over. The memory, which especially haunted literary men, has come down to us until, if we neglect to look up the stark facts, we still think of the Roman Empire as peaceful.

There were, of course, patches of peace and prosperity, particularly in out-of-the-way provinces untroubled by civil war. All over north Africa the population must have increased, for Roman engineers took immense trouble to irrigate more agricultural land and to control sudden floods in the ravines. In Britain and Gaul splendid country mansions, called villas, were built, the headquarters of wealthy estates. They had elaborate central heating, luxurious baths, fine mosaic floors, but they were not the retreats of wealthy men who drew their income from distant investments. They were working establishments. The barracks of slave-laborers were in plain view, just across the courtyard; very often some room in the mansion itself would be set aside as a workshop for the weaving or fulling or dyeing of cloth from local wool. The owner was not an investor, as were most Roman senators; he was a wealthy farmer, busily managing his own land.

In these northern provinces the towns, many of them less than two hundred years old, were already beginning to decay soon after 200 A.D. The natives had built them in a burst of enthusiasm, to prove that they were becoming really civilized; but afterward there was little reason to keep them inhabited. Tribal councils and law courts met within the town, but members of these eminent bodies mostly lived in their villas in the country. Butchers, bakers, carpenters, and smiths could work just as well in a village. A town should be a home of craftsmanship and trade; but in Britain there were few craftsmen, and there was no great desire to swap the local wool and beef for that produced by the neighboring tribe.

Oddly enough, within the Roman Empire there was little long-distance trade, though there were no barriers against it. Small portable luxuries traveled far: fish sauce from Spain, cosmetics from Egypt; and of course the feeding of the populace of Rome meant large shipments of grain. But most craftsmen were slaves, so it was generally easier to open a branch factory in a new market than to supply it with imports from afar. During the reign of Augustus the characteristic Roman tableware, called "Samian," was made mostly in Italy; but potteries were opened in Gaul and Britain as soon as these provinces showed a demand for it. The slave-craftsmen, of course, had to go where they were sent.

The Romans, with plenty of slaves at their disposal, were not interested in saving labor. In Sicily there was a water mill, widely known as an amusing curiosity; but over most of the Empire grain was ground in little hand mills, slowly and with great toil. This grinding was the characteristic task of slave-women, who might spend the whole day doing nothing else. The wealthy classes usually traveled in litters carried by men; to ride without stirrups was uncomfortable, and horse-drawn carriages without springs were even worse. All warships were moved by oars. A whole complicated civilization, whose public undertakings compare with those of today, was powered mainly by the force of human muscle.

Slavery pays very well so long as you can buy, cheaply, plenty of strong docile young men. Under the Republic there had been a plentiful supply of able-bodied captives; the conquest of Sardinia so flooded the slave market that the cry,

"Sardinians for sale," became an expression meaning to try to get rid of worthless goods. During the last century B.C. thousands of Gauls and Germans were brought to Rome. Suddenly, as the frontiers of Rome ceased to expand, the supply ceased. After about 100 A.D. everyone complained of a rising cost of living.

# THE LATER EMPIRE

After the death of Nero in 68 A.D. every emperor felt himself to be short of money. He had to pay his soldiers, and the huge population of Rome expected to be supported in luxurious idleness; but there seemed to be less gold about than there used to be.

This may well have been the case. The old Republic had lived very largely on the plunder of its enemies, including masses of gold from the hoards of Oriental kings. Then, during the reign of Augustus, Rome began to import Chinese silk, of course through numerous middlemen. The flow of gold was reversed, for the Chinese did not want any Roman products; all imported silk had to be paid for in cash. No Roman soldier or merchant could be fobbed off with paper money either; when the government eventually settled a debt it had to pay in silver or gold. At first prices fell, and so did the yield of every tax. The pay of the soldiers remained the same, and as a result they became richer while the central government became poorer. It was probably to increase the number of taxpayers that the Emperor Caracalla, in 212 A.D., abolished the distinction between provincial and citizen.

During the third century A.D. new dangers arose in foreign affairs, which were not the fault of anyone in Rome. The Parthian aristocracy which had ruled Mesopotamia for three hundred years disappeared without trace, and the new native Persian dynasty was more warlike. Within the Empire at this time civil war seldom ceased, for the generals whom the soldiers raised to power were so cruel or so eccentric that many provinces would not obey them. And about the same time the Germans discovered that behind the fortifications of the Rhine and the Danube lay rich and undefended districts. As a result the small Roman army was engaged on three fronts at once: in Gaul, south of the Danube, and in Asia. There were just not enough troops.

The shortage of money suddenly became very grave. Emperors and rebel leaders had to pay their soldiers promptly; but they paid them with little copper coins barely washed with silver on the outside. A soldier who wore a sword could compel merchants to accept these coins, but once in civilian hands the coins lost most of their nominal value. Prices bounded up; no one would lend good money for fear of being repaid in bad. The crisis grew until Rome was practically without a currency. Men ceased to count these worthless little coins; the *follis*, the purse full of small change, became the popular unit of account.

Meanwhile the emperors were too busy fighting on the frontiers to attend to financial matters. The outnumbered Roman army of the Danube won victory after victory, but still the barbarians came on. The Goths—Germans who had taken to cavalry tactics—broke through from south Russia into Greece and sacked Athens; a new confederation of German tribes, the Franks, pillaged Gaul; in the East the Arabs of Palmyra, ostensibly allies of Rome, took over the defense of Syria and Asia Minor but sent no tribute to Italy. For a short time Maximinus, an unusually barbarian emperor, replenished the treasury by plundering all the temples; but such a despoiling of the offerings of centuries could not be repeated. It seemed that the Empire must fall.

Bad times were not quite universal; some distant provinces escaped barbarian invasion. These actually prospered, presumably because wealthy refugees brought in money. In Britain the villas flourished as never before, and in north Africa more land was brought into cultivation. But everywhere taxation was very high, and there were not enough slaves.

The Empire was saved by the great Diocletian, who reigned from 284 to 305. He had done well in the army, for the soldiers named him emperor on the death of his predecessor; but his chief interest was administration.

He changed nearly everything in the Roman way of life. His policy might be called socialism, though without any admixture of democracy. His chief aim was to compel his subjects to work at some task useful to the state, whether they wished to or not, whether they made money by it or not. There was a shortage of food and of many essential services. Therefore Diocletian decreed that anyone who worked on the land must stick to it until he died; even a slave farm-laborer might not be set to any other work by his owner. In the same way bakers must bake, and sailors must manage their ships. The penalty for disobeying this law was death. The sons of forced workers must work at their father's trade, and might marry only the daughter of a man in the same calling.

Diocletian frowned on cruelty to slaves, because it wasted manpower. In any case, if a slave and a free man must work side by side in the fields all day, under pain of death, there

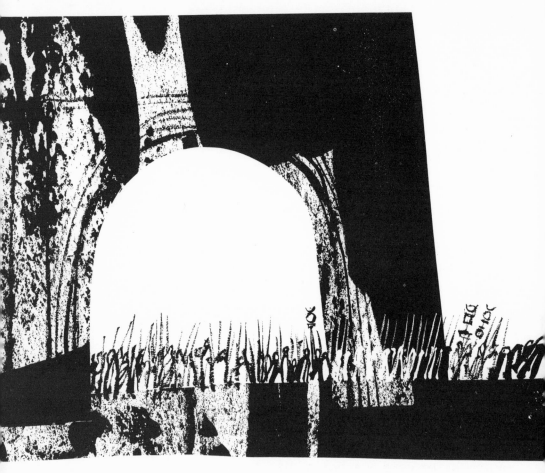

is little distinction between them. The Roman farmer who once had been the backbone of the legions was now dwindling into the serf of the Middle Ages.

Diocletian also remodeled the administration by dividing the civil service from the army. Hitherto a Roman governor had been supreme in every field, responsible for the defense of his province and for its drains. Now the tax collector might not give orders to soldiers, and the general might not

take money out of the treasury. An enormous civil service was required, to keep track of all the forced laborers.

Money was needed above all things. With money one could hire barbarian mercenaries, who fought just as well as Roman soldiers and were not inclined to overthrow emperors. So Diocletian paid particular attention to the collecting of taxes. His subjects were divided, legally and officially, into rich and poor. The tax collector dealt only with the rich, who were held responsible for collecting the taxes of the poor and must make good any deficiency from their own funds. As a result the town councilors were very soon impoverished. They asked to be allowed to sink into the ranks of the laborers, but this was forbidden. Town councilor was now a hereditary caste, like baker or farmer.

In the countryside, away from garrisons of regular soldiers, things worked out differently. Great landowners, after mustering their peasants into private armies, could make a deal with the tax collector. Soon these great landowners, with the soldiers and the senior civil servants, were the only true free men in this vast colony of ants.

After a reign of twenty years, when everything was running to his satisfaction, Diocletian retired to private life. He had already solved the problem of the succession. He himself ruled the East from the great palace he had built at Nicomedia in Asia, while a colleague looked after the West from another great palace in Milan (for the city of Rome, too far from the frontier, was now an unimportant backwater). Each supreme emperor had already chosen a vice-emperor who would step into his shoes.

Diocletian finally abolished the 300-year-old fiction that the emperor was just a Roman noble who happened to be commander in chief. In the elaborate court etiquette he composed, the emperor wore unique garments, which no subject might wear without being guilty of treason; his ministers showed their respect for him by kissing the ground before his feet. Everything reserved for imperial use bore the title of Sacred—the Sacred Wardrobe, the Sacred Palace; most ironical of all, the treasury was known as the Sacred Largesse, because, very rarely, the emperor gave presents from it. But the chief task of the Sacred Largesse was to receive the money of the taxpayer.

In general, the emperor was treated as a god on earth, partly because there were no other universally worshiped gods to rival him. The old sacrifices to Jupiter and Mars still continued, because it might bring bad luck to Rome if they ceased; but practically every Roman who followed any religion at all had chosen a private god. Many soldiers worshiped Mithras, a god of Persian origin whose cult was practiced in secret; there were degrees of honor among his worshipers, as in modern Freemasonry, and to advance to a higher degree cost money in valuable sacrifices. Many townsfolk worshiped the Egyptian Isis, a kindly goddess who was believed to work miracles to help her flock; her cult also was secret and mysterious. Poor countrymen had many local divinities who might be worshiped without costly sacrifice; but there was nearly always at least a secret password to mark off the elect from the profane.

Ever since the Crucifixion, Christianity had been increasing, though always viewed with dislike by the state. Christianity has of course no secret doctrine; every Christian is encouraged to learn as much theology as he can. But in those days there was an element of secrecy in its practice; only baptized Christians might be present at Mass, which made it easy for enemies to spread rumors of scandalous goings on. Persecution had been continuous since the days of Nero, but its intensity varied from time to time. Diocletian, as one might expect, was one of the most savage persecutors.

Diocletian retired to the country house he had built at his birthplace, near modern-day Split in Yugoslavia; a country house so vast that later a city complete with cathedral grew up inside it. Roman official buildings were getting bigger and more elaborate, but there were no more important private mansions—the tax collector had seen to that.

In his retirement old Diocletian lived long enough to see

the total collapse of his system of adoptive succession. In 306 the army in Britain proclaimed Constantine to be emperor. By the year 325 he had conquered the whole Empire. He fought as the patron and ally of the Christian Church, though he himself did not submit to baptism until he lay dying in 337. That was from motives of prudence. He knew that baptism washes away all past sin and he was a very wicked man, treacherous and a murderer of his own kin. But he made Christianity the official religion of the Empire, and his army marched under Christian standards.

This Christian Roman Empire lingered in the East until the Turks took Constantinople in 1453, becoming more Christian and less Roman as time went on. But in the West it was near its end. The policy of hiring barbarians to serve in the army meant that the barbarians went home with a full knowledge of Roman weapons and tactics; and they greatly outnumbered the Roman soldiers. Roman generals held the Rhine against great odds; but there were no reserves behind the front-line troops, and once the fortified frontier had been broken it could never be restored. In 406 the Rhine froze from bank to bank. A great host of barbarians crossed the ice between the fortified bridges, and got into Gaul. They were never expelled.

The Britons found themselves cut off from Rome. Instead of sending help they set up an emperor of their own, who led the garrison of Britain to the conquest of Italy. When the emperor's army was wiped out, the Britons, without regular soldiers, defended themselves against raiding Saxons.

In 410 Alaric the Goth sacked Rome. Barbarian chiefs still found it convenient to keep a tame "Roman emperor" in camp, to give them a legal title to the land they plundered. But in 476 even this pretense was abandoned, and Odoacer the barbarian proclaimed himself "King of Italy."

# THE LEGACY OF ROME

The ancient Romans had a genuine passion for doing justice between man and man, though when they considered disputes between states they were too often blinded by patriotism. But their patriotism was stouthearted and unflinching. The Roman Republic, fighting against more powerful foes, never thought of surrender; when a Roman army had been destroyed in battle there was never any difficulty in raising another. Perhaps a Roman might be too ready to massacre his enemies; but if his enemies gained the upper hand he was ready to face death in his turn. When the war was over, and love of justice could replace love of country, he was usually ready to make a lenient peace, and to observe its terms.

In the Third Punic War the Romans murdered Carthage; the wretched Carthaginians were goaded into fighting after they had lost all chance of successful resistance. But the Carthaginians were themselves a cruel people who would have behaved even worse if they had gained the victory. In the Second Punic War Hannibal was defeated, when success seemed certain, because the cities of Italy were eager to fight for their Roman masters. As an imperial power, ruling foreigners, Rome was more merciful and understanding than any conquering state that had gone before.

There was undoubtedly something coarse and brutal about Roman behavior. The slaughter of gladiators which became the favorite amusement of the Roman people was just plain wicked, and cannot be excused. But these disgusting games came from Etruria, and they were unknown to Rome in the most heroic days of the Republic.

In general the Romans enjoyed the sight of a plentiful flow of blood. Their religious rites entailed not only the slaughter of numerous animals but their subsequent disemboweling to inspect the liver for omens. Many carvings of the beginning of a sacrifice have come down to us; it was a favorite theme of Roman art. We see the victorious general dedicating the first ox to be sacrificed; the beast stands calmly, gripped by strong half-naked men; handsome boys are in attendance; a priest with veiled head recites the opening prayer while all the participants fix their thoughts on divine affairs.

No sculptor has shown us the end of such a sacrifice, say the extraction of the liver from the hundredth and last ox. The altar must have been awash with bloody entrails, everyone spattered with gore from head to foot, the ground carpeted with beef and ox dung, the attendants wearied by plying their axes. Yet it could not have ended in any other scene.

In the most sacred rite of the worship of Mithras the worshiper who was to be received into a higher degree stood naked in a pit below a scaffolding; directly over his head a bull was butchered, so that the blood dripped down between the planks on his naked body; he was literally bathed in the blood of the bull, from head to foot. In any discussion of Roman manners we must make allowance for this positive liking for blood as a fluid.

The Romans' most admirable trait was their devotion to duty. Even at the height of the civil wars very few Romans joined the enemies of their city. In 53 B.C. some soldiers of Crassus surrendered to the Parthians; a full generation later whether such cowards deserved rescue was still a vital topic of political discussion. Romans were expected to fight to the last.

In 79 A.D. Pompeii was overwhelmed by a volcanic eruption. The disaster was amply reported. More than a century ago excavators found the body of the sentry by the town gate. At the time no one had mentioned the death of sentries. There was no point in telling the obvious. Everyone knew that a Roman sentry stood at his post until relieved, or killed.

Courage and discipline were the great Roman virtues, and by practicing them the Romans were able to conquer all their neighbors.

The Romans were also skilled in administration. Though they were not good at figures they were honest in fields where honesty was expected from them, which did not include taking bribes from wealthy provincials. They must have answered letters promptly and put in a fair day's work at their desks, or their Empire could not have endured. They kept the peace; and in disputes between provincials, where no Roman was involved, they judged fairly.

In the things of the mind they were inferior to the Greeks of the Golden Age. But then so are we, and so has everyone else been from the fifth century B.C. to the present day. Their worst fault was to widen the gulf between the gentleman who thought beautiful thoughts in his study and the artisan who put these ideas into practice. But that gulf had been created by the later Greeks, and the Romans found it as part of their Greek education. Their greatest artistic skill was in the use of language.

Latin is rather a blunt instrument, lacking in delicate shades of feeling. Yet the poets of the age of Augustus so modified it that their poems are immortal. In law, in religion, in instruction generally, Latin is still the best medium, because each statement can mean only one thing and there is no room for misunderstanding.

Whether such a thing as Roman art existed at all has been a subject of dispute. Every stone carved in classical Rome seems to have been carved by a Greek, though he may have been a Greek born in Italy. But the Roman patron who paid for it must have had a say in the design, and often it was something that only a Roman would wish to be made; a triumphal arch, for example, or a fortified wall eighty miles long stretching across north Britain.

In philosophy the Romans invented nothing, preferring to live on discoveries made by the Greeks. But they did in fact live on them and by them. Roman philosophers stood out against their emperor to the point of martyrdom, as unswerving as any Christian.

Concerning the physical world around them the Romans were strangely incurious. It was said that long ago some Phoenicians had sailed right around Africa. Any Roman emperor could have sent an expedition to check the story; none bothered. No maps were made of lands beyond the Empire; Tacitus, writing of the Germans, thought Scandinavia was an island. Rumors drifted about of pleasant isles in the Atlantic, presumably the Azores or the Canaries; no one sailed out to find them. Far off to the east lay another civilized empire; but the Romans could not disentangle China from India.

The Romans were stout comrades, good allies in a battle; but not stimulating companions at a party.

These generalizations apply only to the Romans of Rome, a particular nation and race. By the fourth century A.D. the Roman Empire contained anybody and everybody. That horrid ant heap of forced labor and organized bloodshed was better out of the way. In fact nobody wished to preserve it, except the professional soldiers who lived on it. When once the barbarians had pierced the frontier defenses they met with no resistance from the peasantry, except in Britain, whence the central government had already withdrawn. The Welsh fought for their Church, not for any emperor.

Yet the Roman Empire had been an essential stage in the evolution of Western civilization. Western Europe has never lost the idea of a common culture underlying numerous sovereign states, which may be one of the foundations of the modern United Nations. All the West still uses the Roman alphabet, the week of seven days which became a popular reckoning under the later Empire, the Roman months with their Roman names, the Roman year, with its extra day in leap year which was introduced by Julius Caesar. "Congress," "Senate," "President," are all words of Latin origin, and our political theory is based on Roman speculations. The all-weather road, the government-supported school, the right to leave your money to any heir you choose, are all part of our Roman inheritance. It is a very good thing that there was once a Roman Empire—and also a good thing that it exists no longer.

| | ANCIENT ROME | MEDITERRANEAN WORLD |
|---|---|---|
| **B.C.** 1000–500 | | Greek city-states, about 950 |
| | | Phoenicians found Carthage in North Africa, 814 |
| | Romulus founds Rome, 753 Rome ruled by seven kings, 753–509; Senate established | |
| | | Greeks found seaport colonies in southern Italy, around 720 |
| 500–400 | Tarquin, seventh king of Rome, expelled, 509; beginning of Roman Republic Romans devise constitution; Senate and Comitia (assembly) governing bodies; two equal consuls elected | Persian Wars between Greek states and Persian Empire, 500–449 Golden Age of Greek civilization Socrates, 470–399 Plato, 428–348 |
| 400–300 | Rome rules most of central Italy, about 400 Gauls sack Rome, 390; Roman dominion restored by 343 Appian Way, first Roman road, built; Rome comes in contact with Greek culture Alexander the Great conquers Egypt and founds capital at Alexandria, 332 Egypt ruled by Ptolemies, 332–30 | |
| 300–200 | Punic Wars between Carthage and Rome, 264–146 | |
| 200–100 | Publius Scipio, 237–183 Hannibal defeated by Scipio at Zama, 202 Macedonia annexed, 148; Rome gains dominion over Spain, Sicily, Sardinia, Corsica, and northern Africa; Carthage destroyed | |
| 100–I | Tiberius Gracchus killed in Senate, 133; start of civil wars Cicero, 106–43 | Greek cities in decline |
| | Marius reorganizes army; rivalry with Sulla leads to civil war, 88 Crassus defeats slave uprising led by Spartacus, 71 Caesar conquers Gaul and invades Britain, 58–49; defeats Pompey at Pharsala in Greece, 48; dictator of Rome until murdered in Senate, 44 Octavius defeats Antony and Cleopatra at Actium, 31; takes title of Augustus Caesar and becomes emperor of Rome, 27; civil wars end | Caesar defeats Pompey at Pharsala in Greece, 48 Octavius defeats Antony and Cleopatra at Actium, 31; annexes Egypt to Rome |

| | NEAR EAST AND ASIA | WESTERN HEMISPHERE |
|---|---|---|
| B.C.<br>1000–500 | | Peruvian Indian cultures develop from farming settlements |
| | Assyrian power at height, 750 | |
| 500–400 | Buddha in India, about 560–487; Confucius in China, 551–479<br>Persian Empire founded, 546; extends from Mediterranean to India under Darius<br>Babylon falls, 539<br>Persian Wars between Greek states and Persian Empire, 500–449 | |
| 400–300 | | |
| | Alexander the Great, 356–323, conquers Asia to India (Macedonian Empire) | Rise of Maya civilization, about 350 B.C.–300 A.D. |
| 300–200 | | |
| 200–100 | Great Wall of China built, 246–210; unification of Chinese Empire<br>First overland contact between China and Roman Empire under Han Dynasty in China, 202 B.C.–200 A.D. | |
| 100–1 | Parthian Empire (Persia) at its height | |
| | Pompey conquers Mithridates, 66; brings Armenia, Syria, and Palestine and East as far as Caucasus under Roman rule; trade routes between East and West established | |

| | ANCIENT ROME | MEDITERRANEAN WORLD |
|---|---|---|
| **A.D.** | | |
| 1–100 | Reign of Augustus, 27 B.C.–14 A.D., brings peace and prosperity to Roman Empire from Atlantic to Caucasus | Egypt and Africa send grain to Rome; Mediterranean cleared of pirates |
| |    Rhine remains Roman frontier in Western Europe after defeat of Varus, 9 A.D. | |
| |    Golden Age of Latin literature | |
| | Reign of Julio-Claudian emperors (Tiberius, Caligula, Claudius, Nero), 14–68 | |
| |    Arts decline, army loses touch with civilian life, succession of emperors after Nero marked by civil strife | |
| 100–200 | Peaceful reign of good emperors from Nerva to Marcus Aurelius, 96–180 | |
| |    Roman Empire reaches its greatest extent under Trajan, 98–117 | Roman Empire master of Mediterranean |
| |    Hadrian builds wall in Britain, 120–123 | |
| 200–300 | Towns begin to decay in northern provinces; gold supply diminishes | |
| |    Caracalla gives Roman citizenship to all free inhabitants of Empire, 212 | |
| | | Goths break through from south Russia into Greece and sack Athens, 267; Franks pillage Gaul |
| 300–400 | Diocletian institutes reforms in government, 284–305 | |
| |    Prices stabilized; army divided from civil service | |
| |    Empire divided into Eastern rule (with capital at Nicomedia) and Western rule (capital at Milan) | |
| | Constantine the Great, 306–337 | |
| |    Adopts Christianity (Edict of Milan), 313; Council of Nicaea, 325; establishes new capital at Byzantium, renaming it Constantinople, 330 | |
| | Final division into Eastern Roman Empire (Byzantium) and Western European Empire (Rome), 395 | St. Augustine, bishop of Hippo, 396–430 |
| 400–500 | Rome sacked by Alaric the Goth, 410; sacked by Vandals, 455 | Roman African province (except Egypt) lost to Vandals, 5th century |
| |    Romulus Augustulus, last Roman Emperor, deposed, 476; end of Roman Empire in the West | |

| | NEAR EAST AND ASIA | WESTERN HEMISPHERE |
|---|---|---|
| **A.D.**<br>1–100 | Roads run through Roman Empire from Euphrates to English Channel; period of trade and prosperity | |
| | Crucifixion of Jesus, about 29 A.D.; Christianity spreads | |
| 100–200 | | |
| | Roman Empire reaches its maximum extent under Trajan, 98–117; greater part of Parthian Empire, including Armenia and Upper Mesopotamia, conquered | |
| 200–300 | Sassanian Dynasty founded in Persia, 226 | |
| 300–400 | Diocletian rules Eastern Roman Empire from Nicomedia, 284–305 | Maya period of prosperity, 300–700 |
| | Council of Nicaea, 325<br>Constantine establishes new capital of Roman Empire at Byzantium, renaming it Constantinople, 330 | |
| 400–500 | Final division of Empire into Eastern Roman Empire (Byzantium) and Western European Empire (Rome), 395<br>    Roman Empire in the East lingers until Turks take Constantinople, 1453 | |

# A SELECTED BIBLIOGRAPHY

Bailey, Cyril, ed., *The Legacy of Rome*. New York, Oxford University Press, 1923.

Baumann, Hans, *I Marched With Hannibal*, trans. Katharine Potts. New York, Henry Z. Walck, Inc., 1962.

Carcopino, Jerome, *Daily Life in Ancient Rome*. New Haven, Yale University Press, 1940.

Church, A. J., *Roman Life in the Days of Cicero*. New York, Biblo and Tannen, 1959.

———, *Lucius, Adventures of a Roman Boy*. New York, Biblo and Tannen, 1962.

Coolidge, Olivia, *Roman People*. Boston, Houghton Mifflin Company, 1959.

———, *Caesar's Gallic War*. Boston, Houghton Mifflin Company, 1961.

Cottrell, Leonard, *Hannibal, Enemy of Rome*. New York, Holt, Rinehart and Winston, 1960, 1961.

Cowell, F. R., *Everyday Life in Ancient Rome*. New York, G. P. Putnam's Sons, 1961.

Duggan, Alfred, *Julius Caesar*. New York, Alfred A. Knopf, 1955.

———, *Three's Company*, A Novel About the Triumvirate. New York, Coward-McCann, 1958.

Foster, Genevieve, *Augustus Caesar's World*. New York, Charles Scribner's Sons, 1947.

Grant, Michael, and Pottinger, Don, *Romans*. Edinburgh, Nelson, 1960.

Graves, Robert, *I Claudius*. New York, Modern Library, 1934.

Hamilton, Edith, *The Roman Way*. New York, W. W. Norton, 1932.

———, *Mythology*. Boston, Little, Brown, 1942.

Johnston, Mary, *Roman Life*. Chicago, Scott, Foresman and Company, 1957.

Lamprey, L., *Children of Ancient Rome*. New York, Biblo and Tannen, 1961.

Lawrence, Isabelle, *Gift of the Golden Cup*. Indianapolis, Bobbs-Merrill, 1946.

———, *The Theft of the Golden Ring*. Indianapolis, Bobbs-Merrill, 1960.

Mills, Dorothy, *The Book of Ancient Romans*. New York, G. P. Putnam's Sons, 1927.

Pater, Walter, *Marius the Epicurean*. New York, E. P. Dutton and Company (Everyman's Library).

Plutarch, *The Children's Plutarch*, ed. F. J. Gould. New York, Harper and Brothers, 1910.

———, *Ten Famous Lives*, revised and edited for young readers by Charles Alexander Robinson, Jr. New York, E. P. Dutton and Company, 1962.

Shakespeare, William, *Julius Caesar*.

Trease, Geoffrey, *Message to Hadrian*, An Adventure Story of Ancient Rome. New York, Vanguard Press, 1955.

Wagner, John and Esther, *Gift of Rome*. Boston, Atlantic Monthly Press, 1961.

Williamson, Joanne S. *The Eagles Have Flown*. New York, Alfred A. Knopf, 1957.

# INDEX

# ABOUT THE AUTHOR

ALFRED DUGGAN has devoted himself in his writings to bringing to life major figures and important events of the past. His fascination with the classical world began when at the age of twenty-one he and a companion motored from Germany through Italy, Greece, and Yugoslavia, then a daring and even hazardous adventure. Later he was part of an expedition to excavate the original palace of Constantine in Constantinople. His travels have taken him through the Panama Canal to the South Seas—he is one of the few people in recent years to have crossed the Atlantic in a 600-ton barkentine under sail—and many times throughout Europe and the Middle East. His works include *Knight With Armor, The Conscience of the King, The Little Emperors, The Lady for Ransom, Besieger of Cities,* and biographical novels of Thomas à Becket (*My Life for My Sheep*) and Julius Caesar.

Mr. Duggan was born in Buenos Aires but he moved to England at an early age and regards himself as a British subject. He was educated at Eton and Balliol College, Oxford. During World War II he saw action in Norway with the British Army and after a medical discharge worked in an airplane factory. He presently lives in a sixteenth-century house in a rural area of Herefordshire, England, with his wife and son.